High Performance Through Process Excellence

Mathias Kirchmer

High Performance Through Process Excellence

From Strategy to Execution with Business Process Management

 Springer

Dr. Mathias Kirchmer
Executive Director-Business Process Management
Accenture
Two Commerce Square, Suite 2400
2001 Market Street
Philadelphia, PA 19103
USA
mathias.kirchmer@accenture.com

Affiliated Faculty
Program for Organizational Dynamics
University of Pennsylvania
483 McNeil Building
3718 Locust Walk
Philadelphia, PA 19104-6286
USA

ISBN 978-3-642-21164-5   e-ISBN 978-3-642-21165-2
DOI 10.1007/978-3-642-21165-2
Springer Heidelberg Dordrecht London New York

Library of Congress Control Number: 2011935216

Printed on acid-free paper

Springer is part of Springer Science+Business Media (www.springer.com)

Foreword to second Edition

Economic volatility, increasing globalization, rising complexity, and growing interconnectivity have forced businesses to make major changes to their operations in recent years. This trend is likely to continue with change being the new normal and business agility being an absolute imperative to achieving high performance in the future.

At the same time, advances in technology such as cloud computing and service-oriented architectures are creating more flexible and configured application environments that can deliver tremendous value if used in the proper way.

Pragmatic business value–led approaches to Business Process Management are increasingly seen as key enablers in creating transparency of the business environment; managing the complexity of a diverse technology portfolio; and creating the agile link between business strategy and its execution.

Mathias Kirchmer has an exceptional academic background in the understanding of Process Centricity and the methods and tools to support it. By joining the Accenture BPM team, he has mastered the pragmatic business application of these approaches to drive real value. He has also had numerous opportunities to apply this process management know-how in a number of large global clients. It is this experience that has been added to the revised version of this book.

Peter H. Franz
Managing Director – Business Process Management
Accenture
London, July 2011

Foreword

Globalization, speed, and fierce competition are some of the key attributes of the business environment that modern enterprises face each day. Companies must act fast and develop new business models in order to be successful. Innovation and agility are no longer optional, but a crucial capability for companies to survive in the long term.

Business processes are the critical link between strategy and execution. Business process management enables agility within an organization by turning ideas into action. It helps with the development and implementation of new business models across an organization. This book demonstrates how proven practices, like the use of the ARIS Framework, can be successfully combined with new process management developments to achieve the best business value for an enterprise. SOA and Web 2.0 are important hot topics, just like process governance, people change management, reference models, emergent processes, and global inter-enterprise processes. This book combines real-life examples with the newest research findings.

For many years, Mathias Kirchmer worked at the company I founded: IDS Scheer, a leading provider of solutions for business process excellence. His practical experience with numerous companies and the findings of his innovation initiatives are reflected in this book.

August-Wilhelm Scheer
Founder of IDS Scheer
Saarbruecken, Germany
May 2008

Preface to second Edition

The Management of Process Excellence, a value-driven approach to Business Process Management (BPM), has become even more relevant since I have published the first edition of this book. Most of the private and public organizations around the world have started their journey to BPM as reaction to the combination of continuous change in the business environment, new, much more flexible information technology architectures and the maturity level of BPM-related methods and tools. BPM has become a mainstream topic.

I have continued to stay in the middle of this development, now for about 22 years. In the last 4 years, I was fortunate enough to be part of Accenture's BPM Practice, leading the global team focused on BPM-Lifecycle, hence working with organizations to build their BPM capabilities. Working with organizations in North and South America, Europe and Asia, especially India, I could confirm and expand the findings of the first edition of this book. I have also had additional teaching experience at the University of Pennsylvania, Philadelphia, Widener University, Philadelphia (where I gave a computer-based lecture the first time) and the Universidad de Chile in Santiago. The findings during my lectures have been reflected in this second edition of my book.

I would like to thank again August-Wilhelm Scheer for his long year support, mentoring and friendship. His thought leadership has truly shaped the BPM world. It has been a great privilege for me to interact regularly with him. Special thanks also to Peter Franz, Managing Director of Accenture BPM. His leadership, enthusiasm and continuous support have significantly shaped my work in the last 4 years. Thanks also to my long year friend Martin Braun, whose entrepreneurial skills I really admire, Trevor Naidoo, and my academic friends Larry Starr, University of Pennsylvania, Savas Ozatalay, Widener University, Michael Rosemann, Queensland University of Technology, and Sigifredo Laengle, Universidad de Chile. Big thanks also to my clients with whom I had many inspiring discussions, as well as to my colleagues at Accenture, especially the BPM Practice and the BPM-Lifecycle team.

The continuous support and understanding of my wife Monica as well as the encouragement of my family have been of great importance to finish this second edition of the book. Thank you very much for that.

Mathias Kirchmer

West Chester, Pennsylvania, USA

July 2011

Preface

Continuously changing customer and market requirements have become a dominating factor in today's global business environment. To be successful, enterprises have to adapt quickly to new opportunities and threats. They have to take smart decisions and execute fast to move effectively from strategy to operations. Innovation and agility become key success factors for organizations aspiring to become high-performance businesses. Process excellence is the glue that holds everything together.

The management of process excellence (MPE) has become the key enabler of high performance. It leads to a functioning "real-time enterprise" acting successfully in a global economy. MPE links enterprise strategy with people and technology to achieve outstanding operational performance. Technologies like service-oriented architectures (SOA) or Web 2.0 support MPE. Knowledge assets in the form of process reference models increase productivity. Emergent processes are addressed through appropriate management approaches. MPE delivers the necessary business process governance for large organizations as well as for small and medium companies. The resulting next-generation enterprise is ready for long-term success, as part of an effective inter-enterprise collaboration. MPE enables high-performance business.

This book "High Performance Through Process Excellence" discusses trends in the field of process management and how they can be applied in private- and public-sector organizations to achieve high performance. It addresses executives and managers as well as educators and students.

For almost 20 years, I have been working in the field of business process management. My experience results from work in many countries, especially the USA, Germany, France, and Japan while I was with IDS Scheer, a software and consulting company focused on business process excellence. I have been involved with large and small organizations in various industry sectors. For more than 10 years, I have taught process-related classes at several universities, mostly in USA, but also in Europe and Japan. I am an affiliated faculty member of the Program for Organizational Dynamics at the University of Pennsylvania and a faculty member at the Business School of Widener University. These teaching activities helped consolidate my experiences and observations, and forced me somehow to keep my academic knowledge also up to date.

Recently I joined Accenture, which gives me the opportunity to align my expertise in business processes with Accenture's broad experience and continuing high-performance business research. This will ensure that process excellence is a true enabler of high performance for our clients.

I have included in this book some aspects of my three preferred hobbies: jazz, pop art, and food. You will learn for example what business process engineers can learn from jazz musicians. Process governance is applied to restaurant processes. And in the epilogue, I show what pop art has to do with process excellence.

I thank August-Wilhelm Scheer, founder of IDS Scheer, for his outstanding professional, scientific, and personal support. His advice and encouragement have always been of greatest value. Big thanks also to my long year friend and now colleague Martin Braun, as well as to Falko Lameter, CIO of Kaeser Compressors, for many interesting conversations and joint initiatives.

A special thank you for their endorsements of this book goes to Michael Hammer, author of *Reengineering the Corporation;* Bill McDermott, president and CEO of SAP Americas and Asia; Thomas Kurian, senior vice president of Oracle; and Steve Tieman, vice president at Estee Lauder.

Savas Ozatalay, dean of the Widener Business School, and Larry Starr, director of the Program for Organizational Dynamics at the University of Pennsylvania, have helped me to continue my academic work; big thanks to them too. I also thank my former colleagues at IDS Scheer with whom I have had many interesting discussions, especially to Wolfram Jost, Trevor Naidoo, Marc Scharsig, Rafael Blotta, Georg Simon, and Karl Wagner. I am also very thankful for the support and the input from my new colleagues at Accenture, especially Peter Franz, Narendra Mulani, Jim Adamczyk, Brian Wilkinson, Claire Allen, and Terry Corby. Thanks also to Estera Hayes, Chris Burrows, and Phyllis Kennedy for the proofreading, Heidi Brown for formatting the text, and Tom Pepe for helping with some graphical challenges.

Thanks also to Jeff Schaller, a great emerging pop artist, for allowing me to use his painting *Performance Process* in this book. You can see an excerpt on the cover page and the entire painting in the epilogue.

Last, but definitely not the least, I would like to give a very special thanks to my wife Monica. I am sure it was not easy for her to understand why I spent most of my last Christmas vacation with the fine-tuning of this book instead of enjoying the holiday season together. Without her understanding and support, I could not have finished this book project.

Mathias Kirchmer
West Chester, Pennsylvania, USA
May 2008

Contents

Abbreviations

A/P	Accounts payable
A/R	Accounts receivables
ARIS	Architecture of integrated information systems
ASP	Application service provider
B2B	Business-to-business
BAM	Business activity monitoring
Blog	Web log
BPEL	Business process execution language
BPG	Business process governance
BPM	Business process management
BSC	Balanced scorecard
CBT	Computer- based training
CD	Compact disk
CIO	Chief information officer
CPI	Continuous process improvement
CPO	Chief process officer
CRM	Customer relationship management
DoDAF	Department of defense architecture framework
EA	Enterprise architecture
EAI	Enterprise application integration
e-business	Electronic business
EPC	Event driven process chain
ERP	Enterprise resource planning
EDI	Electronic data interchange
EPI	Electronic process interchange
HR	Human resources
IT	Information technology
KM	Knowledge management
KPI	Key performance indicator
m-Business	Mobile business

MDM	Master data management
MPE	Management of process excellence
MRP	Materials requirement planning
PC	Personal computer
PDA	Personal digital assistant
R&D	Research and development
RFID	Radio frequency identification
RM	Reference models
RPV	Resources, process, values
SaaS	Software-as-a-service
SCM	Supply chain management
SCOR	Supply chain operations reference model
SME	Small and medium enterprises
SOA	Service-oriented architecture
SOX	Sarbanes-Oxley
SCOR	Supply chain operations reference model
VRM	Value reference model
VCE	Value chain evolution
WWW	World Wide Web

Chapter 1
Management of Process Excellence: What Is It and Why Do You Need It?

Today, business process management (BPM) is a hot topic. But that has not always been like that – although the concept has been around for over 20 years. When I first moved from Germany to the United States in 1995, I expected that every company would be discussing business processes and BPM. Familiar with the process-orientation books of Scheer [1] and Hammer [2], I was certain that BPM was a hot topic in US business, just as it was in Germany. However, this expectation proved to be an illusion.

I still remember the first time I met the executives of an American manufacturing company. I was so excited to discuss how BPM could help them overcome some of their challenges. But they looked at me and said: "Please implement this software system. Don't waste our time or money with your ideas about business processes. We don't know anything about BPM, we don't want it and we don't need it. So, please discuss those subjects with your academic friends and let's get back to real business here." At that point, I realized that it would not be easy to position the topic of BPM, and it would take quite a bit of "missionary" work before business process orientation would become mainstream.

This situation only began to change around 2000 with the advent of the e-business hype. Suddenly, companies were forced to talk to each other, about how to best organize their collaboration. They had to discuss business processes. It soon became clear that the concept of "process" and BPM is extremely useful and that it can also be applied within an organization to drive high performance. In parallel, the development of methods, tools, and technologies facilitated process-oriented approaches, also helping to push BPM to the forefront. In the last years, it has really become an exciting and mainstream topic – in the United States and all around the world.

Almost everyone talks about business processes. But when you participate in more in-depth discussions, it also becomes clear that many people are unsure what a business process is and what BPM really means. Consequently, many organizations face great challenges in finding the right approach to it, in using process orientation as a management paradigm that really moves an enterprise forward and produces value – immediately. Therefore, this first chapter introduces the basic definitions of

M. Kirchmer, *High Performance Through Process Excellence*,
DOI 10.1007/978-3-642-21165-2_1, © Springer-Verlag Berlin Heidelberg 2011

business process and BPM and presents management of process excellence (MPE), a specific philosophy and approach to BPM. MPE can be used as a framework for value-driven BPM, focused on outcome, not just methods and tools.

In the following chapters, we will discuss various important aspects of BPM and show how they relate to MPE. The goal is to give an overview of important topics and trends in the field of BPM, focusing on the value they provide to various organizations as they pursue high performance.

1.1   What Is a Business Process?

Let us consider a situation that occurred at a company in the machinery industry. I was engaged to support a company-wide process-improvement initiative. At the beginning of the project, the head of the sales department received an award from the company president because he was able to reduce the sales cycle time from 10 days to less than 5. That meant an incoming order was forwarded to the manufacturing department in less than a week. This seemed to be a great success. However, when we later discussed this "improvement" with the head of production, the downside became clear. He explained that he had to organize a team of people collecting the information that had formerly been included in the order sheets coming from the sales department. But because his team did not have close contact with the customer and the engineering department, this collection took a lot of time, often up to 2 weeks.

This means, if you look at the reorganization from a customer's point of view, it takes up to a week longer to get the desired product. The customer does not care if sales activities are fast or slow, he only cares about the total time he has to wait for the product he ordered. At that point, only the effects of a truly business process-oriented approach lead to real improvements.

The term "process" is used in many different ways. Hence it is important to define what we mean when we talk about a business process. A business process is a set of functions in a certain sequence that delivers at the end a value for an internal or external client. Its start is also clearly defined by an external event [1–5]. This definition is visualized in Fig. 1.1.

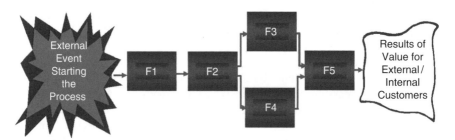

Fig. 1.1 Definition of "business process"

This means every process is a defined subset of an overall organization. Each organizational unit is assigned a responsible person, who is generally called the "process owner." Because the process delivers a value for a customer, its performance can always be measured on the basis of this value. The result is a customer-focused organization because the customer basically sets the metrics by which the process performance is measured. It can react quickly to the market since trends are reflected in changing customer requests.

Every function in a process can again be interpreted as a process by itself, a so-called subprocess. This subprocess is triggered by the previous subprocess (or the overall starting event) and delivers a result of value for the next subprocess (or the final customer and his processes, if it is the last subprocess of an end-to-end process). Such a hierarchical decomposition of a process allows increasingly higher detail of examination of the process [6, 7]. However, the key is to start with an end-to-end view, ensuring an overall process orientation. The decomposition of a process is shown in Fig. 1.2.

I have often been asked how much one can detail the description of a process. This answer is simple – a business process can be decomposed as long as the resulting functions still make sense from a business point of view. The subprocess "handle sales order" may be described in detail using functions, such as "enter sales order." This is the highest level of detail that still makes business sense. Decomposing the last function would result in activities such as "enter name," "enter address," etc. These functions are not relevant from a business point of view.

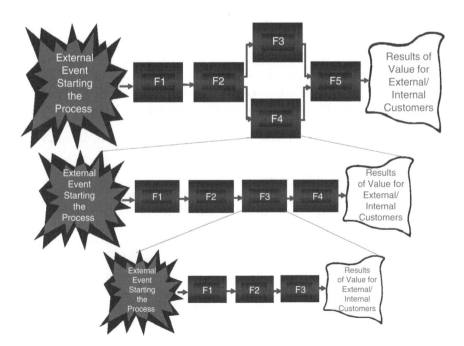

Fig. 1.2 Hierarchical decomposition of a business process

The aforementioned machinery company did not improve the entire business process from the point the customer order arrives (start of the process) until the product is delivered to the client (end of the process with result of value for the customer) but only improved one function (sales), which led to overall lower performance of the entire business process. Such situations can be avoided through a consequent business process orientation.

This leads to an integrated view of an organization. In a process-oriented organization, people always wonder how their work affects that of others. Employees do not just execute one activity, but they contribute to the overall process and its deliverables.

To achieve such a process focus, we must examine more in detail what the components of a process are and how they can be described so that the business process can be managed. Once, I was at an analyst conference that featured a presentation claiming that there was a shift from "electronic data interchange" (EDI) to "electronic process interchange" (EPI). Everyone was excited about that new idea – until someone asked exactly what was exchanged between the companies. What does EPI really mean? To answer such a question, a more detailed analysis of a business process is necessary.

Scheer has done some very valuable work in that field. He has developed an approach to process modeling that has become widely used in practice [3, 4]. It provides a way to describe even complex processes easily without overlooking important aspects. This approach is called "architecture of integrated information systems" (ARIS). It explains that a business process can be described from five different points of view, answering all relevant questions regarding the process:

- Organization view: Who (people, departments, enterprises, etc.) is involved in the process?
- Function view: What functions are carried out within the process?
- Data view: What data (information) are needed or produced in the process?
- Deliverable view: What are the deliverables of the process, why do I need it?
- Control view: How do all those views fit together, that means who is doing what by means of which data to produce which deliverables and in which logical sequence are the functions carried out?

This architecture is shown in Fig. 1.3.

The terms "function" and "activity" are used synonymously in this book. The most important element of ARIS is the control view. It shows how two or more aspects of a process fit together, e.g., who is responsible or accountable for a specific function or which function uses certain data. The resulting integrated view of various aspects of a business process is the key for the successful management of those processes. It helps aligning an organization and makes BPM a real management discipline.

Coming back to our question about EPI, we can now describe what could be exchanged between companies: There may be a shift of organizational units from one organization to the other, a reallocation of functions or deliverables, an exchange of data or a change of control activities between the companies.

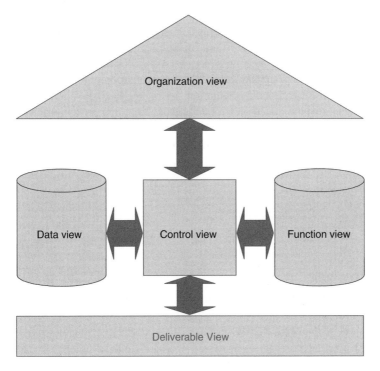

Fig. 1.3 Architecture of integrated information systems (ARIS, after Scheer [3, 4])

If you can answer the "ARIS questions" shown above, then a business process is sufficiently described so that the description can be used to drive a business transformation that improves processes in practice. The description of processes is mostly done through graphical methods [4], ensuring the greatest efficiency and effectiveness.

Examples of business processes include the customer order process from the point of time a customer order enters an enterprise until the required products are delivered (and paid), a maintenance process from the point of time the maintenance order is created until the equipment is maintained or a hiring process from the point of time the hiring request is submitted until the employee is on board or even until this employee retires or leaves.

These examples are operational processes. In other words, their focus is on the execution of the operational tasks of a company. Every organization also needs management processes, which ensure the efficient and effective organization of the operational processes. Examples include the evaluation of employee performance or the process of managing a company's information technology (IT) support. Last, but not least, organizations need governance processes to ensure compliance with overall rules and guidelines. In one example, those processes enforce compliance with legal regulations, general "mega trends," technology developments, or shareholder expectations. The three types of process are illustrated in Fig. 1.4.

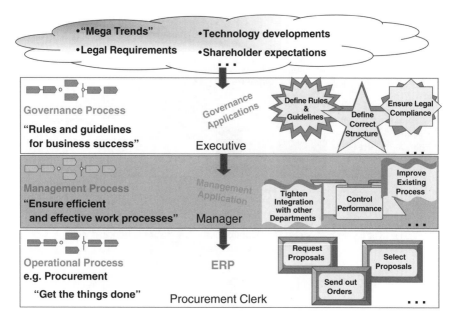

Fig. 1.4 Types of business processes

This classification helps to cover all business processes of an organization in a process management approach. There are many additional ways of classifying processes (e.g., in core and supporting processes). Although these ways may be relevant for specific BPM approaches, we will not discuss them further in this book.

To identify the processes of an organization, one can either use existing industry best-practice models or apply a more analytic approach. Industry best-practice models, so-called reference models, can be applied to a specific company [1, 8]. In other words, the models can be used as a sort of checklist to determine the processes of an enterprise. The use of reference models will be discussed in more detail later.

Another possibility is the analytic identification of processes, using the relevant objects with which a process interacts, especially the products and services of an organization or the targeted markets and channels used [5, 9]. After identification of all market offerings, one defines which processes it takes to sell and deliver those offerings, as well as to manage and govern those processes.

Now we know what a business process is and how it can be described, but what does it mean to manage it? What is BPM all about?

1.2   What Is BPM?

The term BPM is used in various ways in literature and other publications. A useful definition that reflects the philosophy of this book was published by Melenowsky [10]. According to this definition, BPM is a management discipline that provides

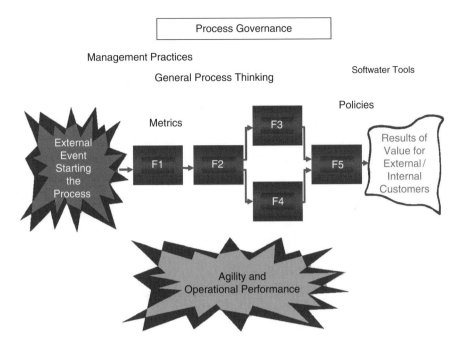

Fig. 1.5 Elements of business process management

governance for a process-oriented organization with the goal of agility and operational performance. Therefore, it uses methods, policies, metrics, management practices, and software tools to manage and continuously improve an organization's business processes. It also requires a general "process thinking," as explained at the beginning of this chapter.

Consequently, approaches like the "agile organization," the "real-time enterprise," or similar concepts are nothing other than the result of the consequent use of BPM. This definition is visualized in Fig. 1.5.

This means BPM is more than just the improvement of a single process. It is more than a single project. Such a focused initiative may be the entry point into BPM, but no more. Also, it is not just about technology. There are more and more vendors in today's market that develop and deliver BPM software. However, that is also only a part of a holistic BPM approach, a building block for the infrastructure. The systematic management of business processes can lead to standardized processes (e.g., in various sales subsidiaries of an enterprise). But BPM does not mean standardization for the sake of standardization. Organizations should standardize when it makes sense for process performance. It also does not necessarily mean the implementation of great changes in an organization. On the contrary, a BPM approach can be used to adjust the size of a change to fit the needs and capabilities of an enterprise.

Naturally, the goal of BPM, used in a value-driven way, is to manage business processes in a way that enables the overall company to achieve high performance.

Accenture research and its work with thousands of companies around the globe has shown that high performance has several building blocks [11]:

- Market focus and position
- Recognize the value of market leadership but do not pursue scale for scale's sake
- Distinctive capabilities
- Makes companies different from their peers
- High-performance anatomy
- Set of mindsets that are observable in decisions and actions, including aspects like innovation and agility, performance measuring, strategic value of IT, people development, leadership

These building blocks can be influenced by an appropriate approach to BPM. According to Spanyi [6], BPM delivers three crucial outcomes for an organization:

- Clarity on strategic direction
- Alignment of an organization's resources
- Increased discipline in daily operations

It is important that BPM focuses on cross-functional processes, as defined before, which always touch internal or external customers. It is not just the management and improvement of subprocesses.

In general, the BPM approach is structured according to the life cycle of business processes [1–6, 8–10]. It can be organized as a process itself: the process of process management [12]. One can roughly distinguish between the activities necessary to build a business process (build-time activities), such as the design and the implementation of a process, and the tasks focused on the ongoing process (run-time activities). As run-time activities, we generally consider the execution of the process (which can be manual through people, automated, or a mixture of both) and the monitoring and continuous management of business processes, including the measurement of key performance indicators (KPIs).

All phases of BPM can be supported by appropriate software systems. In most cases, this is a precondition for an efficient and effective BPM approach. Because of the fact that the phases are integrated, the supporting software must also be integrated, thus entire software suites are used to support BPM, not just single tools to support some of the activities. Those suites support the entire "process of BPM."

We will now discuss MPE and what makes it different.

1.3   What Is MPE and What Does It Add to Business Process Management?

MPE takes a holistic BPM approach and focuses it on achieving the key goals innovation and agility. Hence, it is value driven, focused on outcomes – contrary to more traditional approaches putting methods and tools in the center of BPM. We could just talk about value-driven or outcome-focused BPM [30, 31]. I have chosen in this book to talk about MPE to stress that we move to a new way of using BPM, focused on results and benefits while leveraging the appropriate methods and tools

MPE applies the newest developments in methods, approaches, and IT, and uses them in a consistently business-outcome-driven manner. MPE targets the transfer of strategy into operational performance and value-driven execution delivering innovation and agility. Innovation and agility can lead to revenue and profit growth, cost reductions or in general to additional shareholder value.

Therefore, MPE must achieve two key outcomes in a cost-efficient way:

- Enable smart decisions regarding strategy and operations – in other words, high-quality decisions made in a timely manner
- Ensure the fast execution of the actions resulting from those decisions

MPE not only clarifies strategic direction, aligns resources, and increases discipline but also provides quality information in the required time frame to support the right decisions on all levels of an organization. This information must reflect the entire process, as previously explained. MPE also delivers the infrastructure necessary to ensure the fast execution of resulting tasks. This is essential for a successful enterprise in today's business environment of continuous change. It also enables the rapid correction of errors.

MPE is the critical link between an organization's strategy and execution. It makes the right things happen – quickly. Therefore, it leads to an optimal degree of agility, which supports and encourages innovation. Agility and innovation are the key deliverables of MPE. This specific outcome-oriented definition of MPE makes it different from other, traditional BPM approaches that are mostly more method and tool focused.

If top management of the aforementioned machinery company had realized the impact of their decision on the overall process KPI, they would have modified it to save time and money. However, the fast execution of even a suboptimal decision offers the advantage of a quick correction, if the right performance metrics are in place and measured in the appropriate frequency. In many cases, it is better to come to a quick decision, risking some later corrections, than waiting forever and letting others act.

MPE must ensure the desired results at the lowest cost level, reflecting management's desire to get "more for less" [13]. Hence, efficiency is indirectly address through the focus on "feasible agility." Only the economically feasible approach is relevant in practice. Therefore, MPE requires the use of available standards and best practices wherever possible, based on an approach known as "open BPM" [14]. This "open" approach leads to high flexibility around the process life cycle because of the integration of the various process management phases. This is achieved in a cost-efficient way by using available standards to support the BPM phases, instead of creating methods and tools from scratch on a case-by-case basis.

The MPE approach is shown in Fig. 1.6. It has been developed on the basis of Scheer's ARIS Three Level Framework for Process Excellence [15, 16], a widely used general approach for business process life cycle management. In addition to this and other general approaches [7], MPE places the explicit focus on innovation and agility by linking strategy and execution effectively. This leads to a high-

Fig. 1.6 MPE approach

performance business. MPE underlines BPM's role of enabler for innovation and agility, which has to be reflected in every phase of MPE.

MPE begins with the business process strategy of an organization. The process strategy transfers the overall business strategy into appropriate process structures. First, the main business processes of a company are identified. Next, innovations and their general process impacts are defined, delivering the basis for the definition of the business process structure and the related process goals. Result is a process map identifying a company's end-to-end processes. Innovation areas as well as processes and subprocesses that are especially important to achieve competitive advantage are defined using this process map. The overall goals can be described using concepts like the "balanced scorecard" [17]. The underlying application system architecture is planned accordingly, supporting the required agility. All aspects combined set the guideline and strategic direction for a process-centric organization focused on innovation and agility, driving competitive advantage. The guideline and direction deliver the overall structure for all process-related activities in the following phases of MPE. The process strategy sets the overall governance. The topic process governance will be discussed in Chap. 5.

The strategic guideline is passed to the process design phase, where the business processes are specified in detail. Here, the approach of the "process factory" is used to develop the design as efficiently and effectively as possible to ensure highest agility. This "process factory" concept is discussed in Sect. 1.4. Such a process factory is necessary to ensure a quick move from strategy to the implementation and execution phase while still having sufficient time to focus on process innovations and important strategic improvements. The process descriptions are produced using techniques like simulation, activity-based-costing, or creativity methods in combination with available process-modeling methods. In the design phase, business processes must be specified in detailed and consistent descriptions, which can be used to drive the process implementation and execution. In other words, the created knowledge assets must include all relevant information about the processes to be executed. The result is a process blueprint consisting of business process models that form the enterprise's process knowledge assets and drive the following phases of the business process life cycle.

On the basis of these process models, all physical and information-processing activities are implemented within an enterprise and across organizational boundaries. The results are intra- and inter-enterprise processes, ready for execution. The implementation can be done based on IT to support the following automated execution or manual execution through people. Generally, it is a mixture of both. Some parts of a process may even need to be executed in teams (e.g., brainstorming activities in a research department [18]). This implementation phase includes the software configuration or development, as well as the people change management, including information, communication, and training [19]. For the implementation phase, it is important to have the process blueprint in a format that enables a very time-efficient implementation, so that the execution can start quickly. This can be ensured through the aforementioned process factory. During the implementation phase, the organization goes through a transformation process to achieve the previously defined innovation and agility and with that the targeted competitive advantage.

During the process execution phase, processes are executed on the basis of the implemented IT or people resources. The possible IT support will be discussed in Chap. 3. The software systems can be standard application packages, such as enterprise resource planning (ERP), supply chain management (SCM), or customer relationship management (CRM) systems that primarily support best practice processes. Alternatively, processes can be executed on the basis of more flexible application solutions, such as next-generation business process automation systems, based on a service-oriented architecture (SOA). These alternatives will be described in Chap. 3. The people-based execution may be supported by continuous learning and talent management initiatives, e.g. through computer-based training approaches or regular face-to-face training initiatives. These people aspects will be discussed in Chap. 4. The execution has to deliver the targeted innovation, agility, and other results.

The actual executed processes are measured and controlled in the process monitoring and controlling phase of MPE. If there are negative differences observed between the actual values and the planned KPIs that were defined on the basis of the goals identified in the process strategy, action must be taken. Either a "continuous process improvement" (CPI) is initiated through the process design phase (the design is improved to meet the defined goals and passed on to implementation and then to execution) or the situation is resolved on a strategic level if the business environment has changed significantly. This phase of MPE overlaps with the execution phase. In this monitoring and controlling phase, process performance improvement methodologies, such as Six Sigma [7, 20], Lean or combinations of such approaches [21], can also be implemented. This phase delivers necessary information about the execution to ensure smart decisions, based on process KPIs. It enables a continuous focus on the goals defined in the process strategy and helps to measure drive the success of the implemented innovation and agility. Also new, tool-based approaches like "Process Mining" to discover instances of as-is process can be very useful in this controlling phase [32].

An organization can begin a BPM initiative at any of the phases of MPE. Of course, the typical entry point is process strategy, followed by the analysis and design of processes. However, there are more and more organizations starting with the monitoring and controlling of existing processes, which leads to strategy and process design. The implementation of a process-based software solution can also serve as a starting point. The decision about the MPE starting point should be based on the company-specific situation: the current needs and budgeted initiatives, the political situation, the staffing situation, and similar aspects.

In many cases, companies select a two-step approach and begin with a pilot project focused on one or two processes. On the basis of the result, the entire MPE approach can be rolled out. Whatever starting point is chosen, it is important to envision the entire MPE concept, so every initiative becomes a building block of a successful overall BPM approach.

The design phase, including the process strategy, and the implementation phase comprise the process build-time activities. In this instance, companies must have the ability to act fast to achieve MPE's goal of "fast execution." The process execution, as well as the monitoring and controlling phase, consists of the run-time activities of the process life cycle. They have to deliver the necessary information to ensure timely and high-quality decisions.

All phases of MPE must be supported by available BPM software, as previously mentioned in the general BPM section of this chapter. The data volume to be handled by BPM activities and MPE's specific demand for speed and high-quality information make this request even more important. The necessary integration and consistency of process-related knowledge, especially the business process models, cannot be achieved manually.

A core component of MPE is the aforementioned process factory. It used to support the design phase and helps to organize the link between design and execution. This aspect of MPE will now be discussed in detail.

1.4   The Process Factory: Core Component of MPE

As demonstrated, MPE combines strategic direction with operational execution through IT and people focusing on creating innovation and agility. The whole "process of MPE" (as previously mentioned, the "processes of process management" is also a business process by itself) greatly depends on the efficient and effective capturing and handling of process knowledge in the form of business process models. This can be supported by the approach of the process factory, shown in Fig. 1.7. This approach is based on the storage of the process models in a "process warehouse" (the process repository) and the use of those models to "manufacture" and "assemble" new process models.

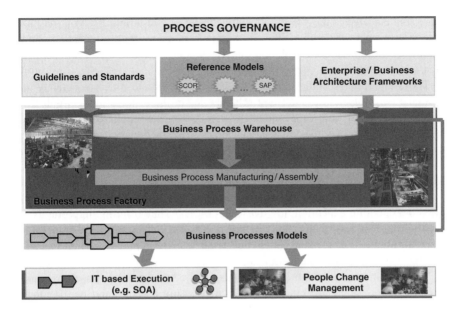

Fig. 1.7 The business process factory

The business process models must be developed and modified frequently to support agility and, with that, a continuous innovation and improvement process. The business process factory is the environment that enables productivity and performance of the management of business process models [22]. It is the critical link between the strategic decision and the fast-operative realization and execution of those decisions that helps enable high performance for the organization.

The design of business processes can be built on the basis of best or common practices. Best practices are available on the market in the form of process reference models (reference models will be discussed in Chap. 6). They are delivered, e.g., by industry organizations, consulting, or software companies [5]. Those models are stored in a database, called the "business process warehouse." The business process warehouse is a repository for all business process knowledge. The best-practice models of the warehouse can be used as "best-practice process components" for the design of enterprise-specific business processes.

In the "process manufacturing and assembling unit," enterprise-specific business process models are "assembled" using available process components, or new processes are manufactured on the basis of the business requirements of an enterprise (e.g., the need for process innovation). The result is generally a combination of best and "next practices" (new, not yet widely established business practices), reflected in the enterprise-specific process models. For straight forward "commodity processes," this step is very simple, since existing process reference models may be used without many or only minor modifications. The more important a process is to achieve competitive advantage, to reach innovation and agility, the more sophisticated is the process "manufacturing and assembling." You may use here improvement techniques like Six Sigma to come up with efficient solutions and combine the modeling with creativity techniques to come up with innovative ideas.

Those enterprise-specific models must be consistent and reflect accurately the desired future business processes. Each mistake in the process models will lead to a mistake in the following implementation and execution phase. Therefore, the simulation of processes, the development and comparison of various scenarios, and a thorough cost and time analysis of the designed processes is extremely important and should be a core component of the process assembling and manufacturing.

In a future "visionary scenario," those process models may be used to create "virtual worlds," which are online environments that allow the user to experience the process before execution, to "live" the process. They offer the opportunity to experience a process change idea before it is rolled out in an organization. The result allows the user to make better educated decisions on process changes as well as a basis for upcoming change management activities [23].

The definition and design of processes must be based on enterprise goals and, from those, deducted process goals. This will ensure a value- and performance-driven approach from the start. Examples of such goals include [5] the following:

- Increased flexibility

    - Cycle time reduction (e.g., of the order-to-cash cycle)
    - Quantity changes (e.g., of production quantities)
    - Product changes (e.g., introduce a new product line)

- Increased quality

    - Product quality (e.g., fewer customer complaints)
    - Support service quality (e.g., hotline support)
    - Information quality (e.g., information about a client's order status)

- Cost reduction

    - HR cost (e.g., overall salaries)
    - Equipment cost (e.g., cost for machines in a factory)
    - Material cost (e.g., cost of necessary raw material)

- Increased revenue

    - Product-related revenue
    - Support-related revenue

- Environmental goals

    - Reduced CO_2 emissions
    - Others
    - Other goals
    - Transparency
    - Reduced risk

It has to be mentioned that the definition of environmental goals will have an increasing importance due to expected legal regulations. Results are so-called "green processes," such as the "green supply chain." Sinur, a well-known BPM expert, even talks about "green BPM" [24].

Process improvement generally begins with the analysis of relevant products (the term "product" is used here in a wide sense, including physical products, services, information products, rights, etc.) [9]. The simplification, change, reduction, or addition of products has significant impact on the defining and high-level design of end-to-end processes. For example, a company producing engineered-to-order locomotives may need one core process starting with the complex sales and engineering of the locomotive, ending with the delivery of and payment for this locomotive. If this company also sells its standardized motors that are produced, but not engineered to order, a second process is necessary. Then the company may decide to also sell its engineering capabilities as a service on the market, leading to another set of processes. Consequently, the structure of the products drives the process design and is, therefore, the entry point to high-impact process improvement. It is of highest importance to reduce the complexity of products as much as possible and keep just that degree of complexity customers are really willing to pay for [25].

Product analysis is fairly straightforward in the field of physical products, such as a car. These products are generally already documented in a structured way, in the form of bills of material. This is an excellent basis for a change of product structure to support simplification or create synergies with other products. In service industries (e.g., banks), the products (services) are usually not as well described. For this reason, it is often more challenging to change and simplify them. Therefore, a specific approach, called "service engineering," was developed in academia and applied in practice, targeting a more systematic development and design of service products [26].

Once the key processes of the organization are identified, they can be assigned to various enterprise levels to define the degree of centralization and decentralization. This can be done using "function-level concepts" [5]. In general, one distinguishes sales-oriented levels (e.g., headquarters, sales region, sales office) and production- or delivery-oriented levels (e.g., headquarters, production location, production center). Once those are defined, you assign the processes and subprocesses to those levels to determine their centralized or decentralized execution.

The product analysis leads to high-level, end-to-end processes. The resulting subprocesses can then be improved via comparison to the aforementioned best-practice reference models and definition of the necessary adjustments or by analytic approaches – analysis of the existing processes.

The analysis of process models, especially models of existing processes, is conducted during "manufacturing and assembling." Here, the business content of the models plays the key role. In most cases, the semantic content cannot be analyzed sufficiently in an automated way. However, the manual analysis can be guided through the ARIS architecture presented at the beginning of this chapter. Weak points of as-is processes may be discovered by applying the structure provided by ARIS and adding the technology aspects, asking e.g., the following questions:

- Organization:

  - Are there too many organizational units involved in the process, causing it to become inefficient?
  - Should additional organizational units be involved (e.g., external units such as customers, suppliers, etc.)?
  - Which external organizational units (e.g., from customers) should be included?

- Functions:

  - Are some of the functions redundant?
  - Is the execution quality of the functions sufficient?
  - Are the functions executed efficiently?
  - Do we need additional functions (e.g., to ensure quality or minimize risk)?

- Data:

  - Is the data quality sufficient (master data, etc.)?
  - Is there redundant data (leading to inconsistencies)?
  - Do we need to adjust the data structure to include relevant information?
  - Do we need additional data, e.g. from external sources?
  - Do we have data that are not really needed in the processes?

- Deliverables:

  - Is the quality sufficient?
  - Do we really need all deliverables?
  - Can we reduce the complexity without negative impact on the value for clients?
  - Do we have to add deliverables?

- Control:

  - Can we make sequential functions parallel?
  - Does the process logic make sense or should we change the sequence of functions?
  - Do we need to centralize or decentralize activities (e.g., found shared service centers)?
  - Should we change organizational responsibilities or accountabilities?
  - Should we change data responsibilities or accountabilities?
  - Is the final responsibility for the deliverables defined?

- Technology

  - Is the degree of IT support appropriate?
  - Is the functionality sufficient?
  - Is the integration sufficient?
  - Does the IT support deliver the necessary flexibility?
  - Is the total cost of ownership of the IT support acceptable?

Whether or not a process design should be changed due to revealed weak points depends on the process goals. For example, if a process has pure quality goals, it may not be worthwhile to invest in eliminating weak points solely related to cycle times. The results of this process analysis and design in the process factory are the models showing the blueprint of the organization.

Those process models are forwarded to the process automation environment (IT-based execution), where they drive the configuration or implementation of the software systems or are used to guide and support the people change management. This ensures process execution according to the developed process design. A holistic business process design drives technology and people to the right direction, resulting in high performance for the organization as a whole.

The process models are stored in the process warehouse, which allows later reuse. Such reuse could include the following:

- Roll out of a process solution to other locations
- Support of mergers and acquisitions
- Selection of software packages on the basis of the business process requirements
- Quality improvement initiatives
- Risk management initiatives
- Additional process improvement initiatives
- Enterprise integration activities (e.g., those related to customers or suppliers)
- Enterprise transformation initiatives, including implementation of new operating models
- Compliance management

The reuse of created business process assets is a very powerful component of MPE, enabled through the process factory. It makes new process initiatives more efficient than preceding ones, ultimately leading to the continuous improvement of "BPM processes." Every reuse increases the delivered value.

Process governance, which will be discussed in detail later, delivers the guiding parameters for the process factory: the reference models to be used (e.g., reflecting the capabilities of a certain ERP system), general guidelines (e.g., about responsibilities and accountabilities), and information about the structure in which the process models will be stored (enterprise or process architecture).

The physical realization of this process factory can occur through the use of process design environments [27] as part of the overall MPE approach. The integration of some of those environments into execution software systems is very important for a fast implementation. For example, the ARIS Platform (software built based on the ARIS Architecture)[28] is integrated into process automation environments (SOA and others), such as SAP NetWeaver, Oracle Fusion, or solutions from other, even smaller process execution software vendors [14, 29]. This enables the seamless handover of the process models and their reuse in the IT execution environments to at least partially automate the configuration or software development. The same process models can be transferred into people-friendly formats to support change management activities. This results in a significant reduction of the implementation time, thereby providing a tight link of an enterprise's strategy and design with its operations.

MPE, with its process factory, is a framework that enables the use of BPM methods, tools, knowledge, and approaches in a business value-driven manner to support the highest-possible performance of an organization. It allows for smart decisions and fast execution of the resulting actions at the lowest possible cost level. MPE is the critical link between strategy and operation, delivering innovation and agility as organizations pursue high performance.

In the following chapters of this book, specific aspects of MPE will be discussed. New BPM developments and trends as well as their impact on MPE are presented. The goal is not to describe every activity within the MPE approach, but to highlight key aspects and provide know-how on topics not already discussed in numerous BPM-related books. At the beginning of each chapter, the MPE phases or aspects of focus are indicated.

In the following chapters, we will start with the discussion of the relation between process management and innovation. This is important to understand why innovation is a key goal of MPE. The IT and people-related aspects of MPE will then be presented more in detail. Once those basic aspects are clarified, the process governance for MPE is discussed followed by a presentation of the concept of "reference models," which are of highest importance for MPE. Inter-enterprise processes and emergent processes require special management approaches. It is shown how MPE approaches those processes. This is followed by a presentation of the impact of globalization on MPE and a discussion of the specific situation of small and medium enterprises. The book ends with a chapter showing what Jazz has to do with MPE. In the epilog, you will then have the opportunity to find out more about process management and Pop art.

1.5   The Bottom Line

- A business process is a set of functions in a certain sequence that ultimately delivers value for an internal or external client. Its start is defined by an external event (Sect. 1.1).
- Every process is a clearly defined subset of an overall organization, managed by a "process owner" (Sect. 1.1).
- Because the process delivers a value for a customer, its performance can always be measured, based on this value. The result is a customer-oriented organization (Sect. 1.1).
- Key views to describe a business process are the organization, function, data, deliverable, and control views (Sect. 1.1).
- BPM is a management discipline that provides governance for a process-oriented organization with the goals of agility and operational performance (Sect. 1.2).
- BPM uses methods, policies, metrics, management practices, and software tools to manage and continuously improve an organization's business processes (Sect. 1.2).

- BPM links strategy and operations of an organization (Sect. 1.2).
- The key outcomes of BPM are clear strategic direction, alignment of resources, and increased discipline in daily operations (Sect. 1.2).
- BPM is a process in and of itself. It can be supported by appropriate software systems to make the approach efficient and effective (Sect. 1.2).
- MPE takes the elements of a general BPM approach, and uses them in a consistently business value-driven way to enable high performance for the organization as a whole (Sect. 1.3).
- MPE targets the transfer of strategy into operational performance delivering innovation and agility (Sect. 1.3).
- MPE supports smart decisions (timely, high quality) and fast execution of the resulting actions at the lowest possible cost level (Sect. 1.3).
- MPE begins with a business process strategy that leads to the process design, implementation, execution, monitoring, and controlling phases. It manages IT-related aspects, as well as people aspects (Sect. 1.3).
- MPE is heavily dependent on an efficient and effective capturing of process knowledge in the form of business process models. This can be supported by the approach of the process factory (Sect. 1.4).
- The process factory includes the process warehouse, a repository that enables the efficient reuse of process knowledge assets. It is an important aspect to ensure MPE's overall efficiency and effectiveness (Sect. 1.4).
- The improvement of processes is based on the achievement of business goals. The first step is generally an analysis of products and their structure because they drive the process definition. The analysis of the detailed subprocesses can be done on the basis of the key process views and the related execution technologies (Sect. 1.4).

References

1. Scheer, A-W: Business Process Engineering – Reference Models of Industrial Enterprises, 2nd edn. Springer, Berlin (1994)
2. Hammer, M, Champy, J: Reengineering the Corporation. Harper Collins, New York (1993)
3. Scheer, A-W: ARIS – Business Process Frameworks, 2nd edn. Springer, Berlin (1998)
4. Scheer, A-W: ARIS – Business Process Modeling, 2nd edn. Springer, Berlin (1998)
5. Kirchmer, M: Business Process Oriented Implementation of Standard Software – How to Achieve Competitive Advantage Efficiently and Effectively, 2nd edn. Springer, Berlin (1999)
6. Spanyi, A: Business Process Management is a Team Sport – Play It to Win! Anclote Press, Tampa (2003)
7. Harmon, P: Business Process Change Management – A Manager's Guide to Improving, Redesigning, and Automating Processes. Morgan Kaufmann, San Francisco (2003)
8. Porter, M: Competitive Strategies: Techniques for Analyzing Industries and Competitors. Free Press, New York (1998) (Originally published in 1980)
9. Kirchmer, M: Market- and product-oriented definition of business processes. In: Elzina, D J, Gulledge, T R, Lee, C-Y (eds.) Business Engineering, pp. 131–144. Kluwer, Norwell (1999)
10. Melenowsky, M.J.: Business process management as a discipline. Gartner Research, 08/2006

11. Cheese, P, Thomas, R J, Craig, E: The Talent Powered Organization – Strategies for Globalization, Talent Management and High Performance. Kogan Page, London/Philadelphia (2008)
12. Kirchmer, M.: The Process of Process Management: Delivering Sustainable Business Value Through BPM. Accenture Point of View Document. Philadelphia (2011)
13. Spanyi, A: More for Less – The Power of Process Management. Meghan-Kiffer Press, Tampa (2006)
14. Kirchmer, M.: Knowledge communication empowers SOA for business agility. In: The 11th World Multi-Conference on Systemics, Cybernetics and Informatics, Proceedings, vol. III, pp. 301–307. Orlando, 8–11 July 2007
15. Jost, W, Scheer, A-W: Business process management: a core task for any company organization. In: Scheer, A-W, Abolhassan, F, Jost, W, Kirchmer, M (eds.) Business Process Excellence – ARIS in Practice, pp. 33–43. Springer, Berlin (2002)
16. Kirchmer, M, Scheer, A-W: Business process automation – combining best and next practices. In: Scheer, A-W, Abolhassan, F, Jost, W, Kirchmer, M (eds.) Business Process Automation – ARIS in Practice, pp. 1–15. Springer, Berlin (2004)
17. Kaplan, R, Norton, D: The Balanced Scorecard – Translating Strategy into Action. Harvard Business School Press, Boston (1996)
18. Harmon, P.: A new type of activity. In: Business Process Trends (ed.): Newsletter 5(19) (2007)
19. Kirchmer, M, Scheer, A-W: Change management – key for business process excellence. In: Scheer, A-W, Abolhassan, F, Jost, W, Kirchmer, M (eds.) Business Process Change Management – ARIS in Practice, pp. 1–14. Springer, Berlin (2003)
20. Snee, R, Hoerl, R: Leading Six Sigma – A Step-by-Step Guide Based on Experience with GE and Other Six Sigma Companies. Prentice-Hall, Upper Saddle River (2003)
21. George, M L: Lean Six Sigma for Service – Conquer Complexity and Achieve Major Cost Reductions in Less Than a Year. McGraw-Hill, New York (2003)
22. Kirchmer, M, Brown, G, Heinzel, H: Using SCOR and other reference models for e-business process networks. In: Scheer, A-W, Abolhassan, E, Jost, W, Kirchmer, M (eds.) Business Process Excellence – ARIS in Practice, pp. 45–64. Springer, Berlin (2002)
23. Greenbaum, J.: SimEnterprise: the video gamer's guide to SAP's business-process revolution. In SAP NetWeaver Magazine, vol. 2 (2006)
24. Sinur, J.: It's time to consider green BPM. In: Global360 (ed.): Jim Sinur's BPM, www.global360.com (2007)
25. George, M L, Wilson, S A: Conquering Complexity in Your Business – How Wal-Mart, Toyota and Other Top Companies Are Breaking Through the Ceiling on Profits and Growth. McGraw-Hill, New York (2004)
26. Bullinger, H.-J., Scheer, A.-W.: Service Engineering – Entwicklung und Gestaltung innovativer Dienstleistungen. In: Bullinger, H.-J., Scheer, A.-W. (ed.): Service Engineering - Service Engineering – Entwicklung und Gestaltung innovativer Dienstleistungen. Springer, Berlin/Heidelberg (2003)
27. Blechard, M.: Magic quadrant for business process analysis tools, 2 H07-1 H08. In: The Gartner Group (ed.): Research Publication G00148777, 6/8/07
28. IDS Scheer A.G. (ed.): ARIS Platform. Product Brochure. Saarbruecken (2007)
29. Newman, D.: BPM & SOA: real world stories of business success. In: IQPC (ed.): Proceedings of the Business Process Management Summit, Las Vegas (2007)
30. Franz, P., Kirchmer, M., Rosemann, M.: Value driven Business process Management – Which values matter for BPM. Accenture, Queensland University of Technology (QUT) White Paper, London, Philadelphia, Brisbane (2011)
31. Kirchmer, M.: Competitive advantage is an end of change: 11 Typical situations where Business Process Management delivers Value. Accenture Point of View Document. Philadelphia (2011)
32. Kirchmer, M., Gutierrez, F., Laengle, S.: Process Mining for Organizational Agility. Industrial Management January/February 2010

Chapter 2
Innovation: An Important Goal of MPE

Today's business environment is constantly changing – new opportunities and challenges arise every day. Achieving and sustaining high performance has become more and more difficult. New competitors emerge from all around the world, while others disappear. A company becomes a member of many enterprise networks, resulting in more changes and additional competitive situations. Fingar, a well-known BPM expert, introduces "extreme competition" as a result of the following five driving market forces [1].

- Knowledge as business capital: The right kind of knowledge is a key asset for competitive leadership and long-term survival.
- The Internet: It enables new dimensions of efficiencies and efficacies in collaboration, traditional supply chains are undergoing transformations from "value chains of knowledge," and information can even replace physical goods.
- Jumbo transportation: Although the Internet connects knowledge workers around the world, "extreme logistics" (new, larger airplanes, ships, etc.) integrate the physical side of business activities.
- Three billion new capitalists: Countries such as India and China are no longer just places to conduct offshore work – they have become powerful members of the economic world.
- The new IT: Technology-enabled BPM will be essential for developing competitive advantages.

To master the resulting challenges, innovation – especially business process innovation – has become a core focus area for successful organizations. To ensure long-term survival, an enterprise must make innovation part of day-to-day business. Only then can enterprises attain desired revenue and profit stability, and growth and high performance.

Two major forms of innovation can be distinguished: business model innovation and technology innovation. Both require the change of existing or the development of new business processes. Business process innovation is a major success factor for the next-generation enterprise. Companies need to create an environment that encourages and enables process innovation. Business process management (BPM)

M. Kirchmer, *High Performance Through Process Excellence*,
DOI 10.1007/978-3-642-21165-2_2, © Springer-Verlag Berlin Heidelberg 2011

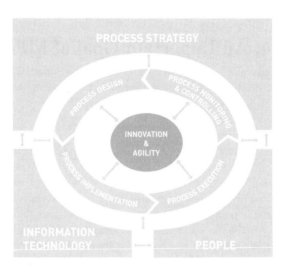

Fig. 2.1 Focus on deliverables of MPE

has to become the facilitator of innovation initiatives, which is reflected in the MPE approach. Innovation and agility are the main goals of MPE.

MPE also applies the philosophy of "Open BPM." This concept delivers a business process infrastructure that provides optimal flexibility at the lowest cost level through the use of business and technology standards. Open BPM enables agility, and, in turn, efficient and effective business process innovation [2].

This chapter discusses characteristics of innovation and the necessary agility. It explains the importance of process innovation for all forms of innovation. You will learn how MPE serves as an enabler for business process innovation. Consequently, the main focus of this chapter is the key deliverables of MPE: innovation and agility. This is closely related to aspects of the business process strategy (where goals and innovation objectives are defined), which influences the entire MPE approach in all phases. This chapter's focus on the MPE deliverables is visualized in Fig. 2.1.

2.1   What Has Innovation to Do with Business Processes?

Today, more and more companies are built on the principles of process innovation. Dell, e.g., did not invent the PC. But it did invent new business processes to bring PCs to market, eliminating unnecessary steps in the supply chain, while offering more flexibility and control to the customer. These processes have become Dell's main differentiator in the competitive marketplace. Process innovation was the basis for starting and growing this company. Amazon.com did not invent the book, but it introduced a now-popular process of buying books online from the comfort of your living room. This is a process innovation based on the Internet with its new technical capabilities. In a further innovation step, they became a broader online retailer. And now they offer their retail platform to other companies so that they can sell new products online. eBay did not invent the auction, but its online, easy-to-use processes increased the popularity of the auction. This is again a process innovation as the basis for a new business.

Traditional companies are also focusing on process innovation. For example, enterprises in the machinery industries offer more convenient and reliable service processes based on Internet connections to their clients or directly to the delivered equipment. Airlines have simplified the ticketing process to reduce cost and increase, or at least stabilize service levels through online ticketing. This is a process innovation that eventually became the standard, an industry best practice. Banks reduce cost and improve their service levels through online banking.

These significant impacts of business process innovation are shown in Fig. 2.2.

Business process innovation is clearly of the highest importance for every company. But what is it all about? How do "innovation" and "business processes" really fit together? Innovation is defined as the act of "introducing something new." A useful structure of innovation is proposed by Davila et al. [3]. According to them, innovation has two major directions:

- Business model innovation
- Technology innovation

Business model innovation includes a new or modified value proposition, new business processes (especially in the supply chain), or new target customers and markets. Let us look at a few examples. Levis Strauss & Co. introduced denim jeans.

Because of the company's new process of putting rivets in pants for strength, jeans were introduced as working clothes for farmers and factory workers. Since the first introduction of the denim jeans, the company's value proposition has changed and evolved, as denim jeans have become an expensive fashion product. In its PC offerings, Dell's value proposition was the convenient custom configuration and ordering of products – the supply chain processes eliminated dealer networks and

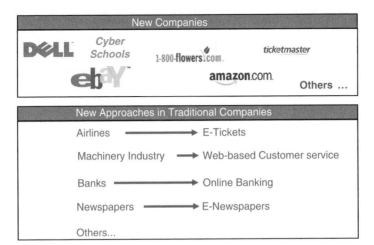

Fig. 2.2 Results of business process innovation

enabled individual configuration by the client, while the target customers remained, more or less, the same as those of competitors. The opening of new markets for existing offerings is another kind of business model innovation. If a company has always sold to US market, but now decides to also deliver products to Europe, this is a form of business model innovation (new market). Sometimes the profit formula is considered as an additional component of the business model; however, it may also be seen as part of other elements (e.g., aspect of the general value proposition).

Technology innovation has the following levers: offerings, including products and services; process technologies; and enabling technologies. New product technologies (e.g., the introduction of digital cameras) are some of the most obvious forms of innovation. Process technologies support efficient and effective business processes. ERP systems, e.g., were able to make specific processes more efficient and effective. Supporting technologies improve either product or process technologies. For example, the development of efficient relational databases supported the development of integrated application software, especially the aforementioned ERP systems.

Innovation in the fields of processes and process technologies show the direct link between "process" and "innovation." But the other forms of innovation also lead to new processes. New value propositions and expansion into new markets require appropriate business processes. A product innovation generally leads to new production or distribution processes. The result is an indirect link between "business processes" and "innovation." Basically, any form of innovation requires new or modified business processes and needs business process innovation: processes with new structures, more accurate, granular or timely data, new organizational responsibilities, new functions or superior process deliverables.

The levers of innovation are shown in Fig. 2.3. The close relationship between innovation and business processes is reflected in various innovation theories that are

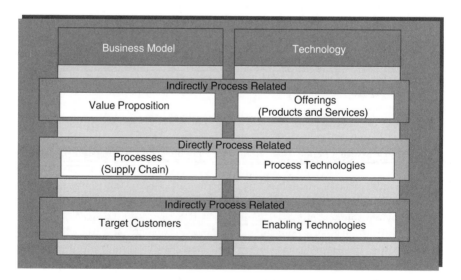

Fig. 2.3 Levers of innovation and the relation to processes

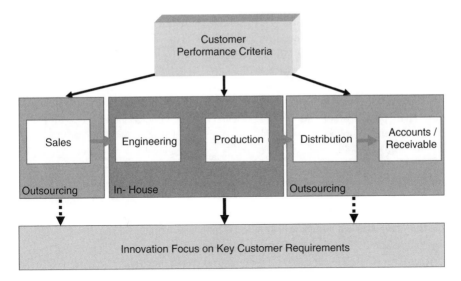

Fig. 2.4 Value chain evolution (VCE) theory

applied in practice, such as Christensen's "Value Chain Evolution" (VCE) theory
and his "Resources, Processes, Values" (RPV) theory [4, 5]. Christensen is one of
the leading innovation experts. The VCE theory is defined around a company's
value chain, which is the process beginning with marketing and sales and ending
with product distribution and accounts receivables. Customer preferences strongly
influence an enterprise's determination of which parts of the value chain process are
outsourced and which are executed in-house. The more important the process steps
are to the customer, the more likely the enterprise will execute the related process
parts in-house. Innovation initiatives are focused on the subprocesses executed
in-house, indirectly leading to an innovation focus on key customer requirements.
Consequently, business process outsourcing decisions also drive the focus of
innovation decisions, especially regarding process innovation. The VCE theory is
visualized in Fig. 2.4.

Christensen distinguished between sustaining and disruptive innovation. Sustaining innovation strives to improve existing offerings. In that way, "undershot
customers," or customers for whom the current offerings are insufficient, can be
reached. Disruptive innovation targets "overshot clients" or completely new
markets. "Overshot clients" are clients who are not interested in the expensive
features of the currently offered products. The present offerings are too sophisticated for them. This distinction is visualized in Fig. 2.5.

The RPV theory demonstrates that innovation is significantly influenced through
a company's resources, processes, and values. Resources are transformed through
processes from an input to an output. Company values are the basis for setting
priorities, thus determining how to use the resources. Successful companies have
developed and combined resources, processes, and values to clearly focus on the
existing offerings that currently make the organization successful. The result is

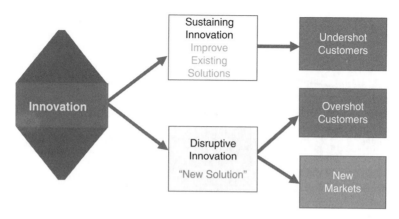

Fig. 2.5 Sustaining and disruptive innovation

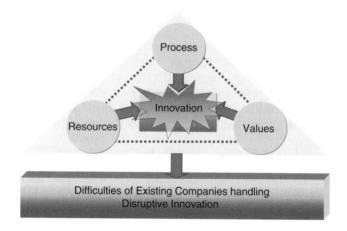

Fig. 2.6 Resources, processes, values (RPV) theory

a sustaining innovation that constantly improves existing offerings. But those companies often lose the agility to do something completely new, something that does not simply sustain their existing products. Therefore, if other enterprises introduce disruptive innovations, focusing on new market segments with new solutions, the existing companies are faced with tough challenges. Their focus on sustaining innovation and their lack of flexibility make it difficult to react to disruptive innovation. Their business processes are generally not agile enough to deal with the wide impacts of disruptive innovation or to produce innovations that are really addressing new markets. In this instance, a BPM approach resulting in agile business processes (enabling process innovation) can become an important factor for long-term survival. The RPV theory is shown in Fig. 2.6.

"Collaboration innovation" is an extension of business process innovation. In this case, inter-enterprise processes are implemented to support "innovative" collaborations between organizations [6]. For example, ING is a bank that works together with coffee shops. When customers visit an ING location, they feel like they are in a coffeehouse – with some terminals in the back for banking transactions. Therefore, the BPM infrastructure has to support this collaboration between organizations. Processes of different organizations must be integrated to deliver value to the final client. Thus, process innovation is again the underlying principle of that new form of collaboration. We will discuss inter-enterprise processes and their BPM requirements later.

An important and very specific form of process innovation is the innovation of service processes. A service as rendered by a consulting company, financial services company, etc., is also a process. That means the "product" they deliver to the market is a "business process." Therefore, the innovation of the offering (the service) must be a process innovation – which is consumed directly by the customer. Product innovation in a service company is essentially always process innovation. Therefore, process innovation in such enterprises is even more of a core focus of their activities.

It is now clear that innovation, especially business process innovation, is a topic that every organization should address. But how can this innovation be organized? How can BPM in general and MPE specifically support business process innovation?

2.2 What Is the "Business Process" of Innovation?

How does an enterprise organize innovation? Once again, the answer is BPM: the management of innovation within an enterprise is a business process in and of itself. This process must be defined, implemented, executed, and controlled just like any other business process. It goes through the same process life cycle and can be managed using the MPE approach. The "innovation process" is a key process to be managed by MPE.

An example of one such innovation process is shown in Fig. 2.7. The process develops from the preparation of an innovation initiative, to the "idea finding" activities, and finally to the execution of the innovation idea. The innovation manager identifies relevant mega trends and, on the basis of those, the relevant innovation fields. These innovation fields guide the definition of the company-specific innovation focus. This focus directs the "idea finding," using internal and external resources. The innovation ideas are evaluated, and the most interesting ones become innovation projects. These projects develop prototypes and business cases on the basis of the innovation idea. Then, the innovation team can decide which innovation ideas will be brought to market, or the ideas that will actually become innovations.

During the idea-finding process, it is the key to anticipate the customers' future interests and needs. Fingar claims that you should even know these interests and needs before the customers themselves are aware of them [1]. It generally makes

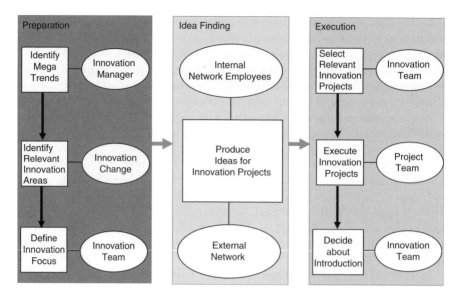

Fig. 2.7 Example of an innovation process

sense to include external partners in the innovation process to broaden the input. Examples of such partners include the following:

- Key customers
- Important suppliers
- Additional market partners (e.g., banks)
- Research institutions
- Universities

Generally, the subprocess resulting from idea finding is an emergent process, which cannot initially be defined from start to finish. Later, we will discuss how to manage these processes.

In most cases, however, the step from the idea to the innovation itself is the most challenging. Therefore, the management of innovation projects and their evaluation is a key activity in the innovation process. An organization can truly achieve competitive advantage by organizing that activity in a successful, company-specific manner.

Because of the importance of process innovation, the innovation process must support this form of innovation effectively. For many traditional companies, this will require a big shift because they formerly thought of innovation in terms of technology innovation, especially product innovation. This shift can be supported by selecting the appropriate external partners to participate in the innovation process.

Davila, Epstein, and Shelton suggest some rules to support and manage the innovation process [3]:

- Implement strong leadership regarding innovation strategy and portfolio
- Integrate innovation into day-to-day business
- Align amount and type of innovation with the specific business situation
- Manage tension between creativity and daily business requirements ("achieve numbers, etc.")
- Control the resistance to innovation and change
- Form an innovation network consisting of internal and external members
- Define and manage the appropriate metrics and rewards

When implementing and improving an innovation process, it is of highest importance to accelerate the time until the innovation can be introduced into the market. This reduces innovation cost and increases the probability of high revenue effects [7, 8]. The innovation process is designed to create something new. Consequently, you will discover new facts while executing the processes that may lead to process changes and adjustments. The innovation process is often an emerging process [8], a topic we will discuss in Chap. 9.

Hammer, the renowned BPM thought leader, recognized that operational innovation, or business process innovation, is not easy to achieve. For a successful innovation process, he recommends six key factors [9]:

- Business process focus, from the beginning of an innovation initiative
- Definition of process owners, including a senior executive who can make change happen
- Full-time design team
- Managerial engagement, ensuring the implementation of the innovation
- Building buy-in
- Bias for action

Once a process innovation has been implemented, one must recognize that the interrelation with other processes may require additional change. Therefore, one process innovation initiative may immediately trigger the next process change project.

The innovation process can be centralized in an organization or carried out in decentralized units. The more effective approach has to be defined on the basis of a company's specific strategy. This is especially true for organizations working in a global business environment, an important topic [10]. The topic will be discussed on a general level in Chap. 10.

How can an enterprise provide an environment to support this innovation? How can MPE facilitate the innovation process?

2.3 How Does MPE Support Innovation?

MPE provides a business infrastructure with the flexibility necessary to facilitate innovation, especially business process innovation. It sets the parameters so that an organization is able to react to change efficiently and effectively. Process innovation is simply a special driver of such change.

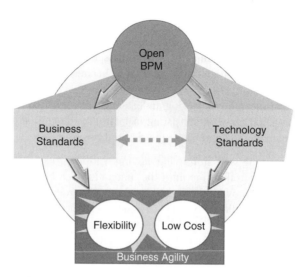

Fig. 2.8 Concept of open business process management

As previously mentioned, MPE applies the notion of "open BPM," which is the consequent use of business and technology standards around the process life cycle, resulting in an infrastructure that provides optimal process flexibility at the lowest cost level. The use of standards to support process management allows business process changes (e.g., regarding the design of a process) with minimal effort because the information about the change can be seamlessly transferred to all phases of the process life cycle (e.g., to ensure the necessary IT support and execution of the new process). The resulting flexibility is the key enabler for business process innovation. The concept of open BPM is shown in Fig. 2.8.

Some BPM software and solution vendors and other organizations choose a "closed" approach to BPM, or use proprietary solutions that do not support standards. This reduces the flexibility to change because of missing integration between the phases of a process life cycle, especially between design, implementation, and execution. Therefore, a closed approach would not facilitate innovation. The concept of MPE cannot be implemented, based on closed concepts – it requires a strategy of open standards.

To achieve the greatest possible number of benefits, the philosophy of open BPM must be applied to each phase of MPE. On the one hand, all phases of MPE must be organized from a business point of view, requiring adherence to the "process of MPE." On the other hand, the required methods and software support must be provided, as explained earlier. The use of open standards for all business and IT aspects of this business process life cycle management is necessary for organizations to reap the full benefits of Open BPM.

Business standards that can be applied to guide the process design include architecture standards like the SCOR framework developed by the Supply Chain Council, the ARIS Architecture developed by Scheer, or the Zachman Framework

[11, 12]. Processes can be described using modeling standards, such as event-driven process chains (EPC) [13].

The execution of processes in an open environment is best supported by SOA [14, 15], a highly flexible next-generation process automation that will be later discussed in more detail. The process-design information describing the business situation can be transferred into technically oriented standards, such as the Business Process Execution Language (BPEL) [16]. The BPEL (or similar standard-based) process models are loaded into the technical middleware of SOA, which is then configured based on the process information. The application software components, or the "services," are utilized according to process needs. This leads to truly process-oriented application software – with very flexible configuration capabilities, so that changes in process design can be reflected very quickly. These technology standards directly deliver the agility necessary to drive process innovation. These IT-related aspects will be discussed further later on.

The main activities of people change management are information, communication, and training. These activities can be supported by the same process models, provided that a consistent process-modeling standard is used, such as the aforementioned EPC. Such formal process-modeling methods can be transferred into process descriptions that are easy-to-understand and easy-to-use, even for less-skilled employees. Change management encompasses the people side of process execution. Maximum flexibility in the technical execution of processes requires equal flexibility from the people working directly or indirectly with those technologies. Also, the people change management will be presented more in Chap. 4.

Process-controlling systems can be linked to the SOA (or traditional process automation environments) through standardized adapters to monitor and measure the business processes [17]. Information, such as cycle times or execution frequency, is monitored. Thus, it becomes easier to provide real-time information about potential process issues so that appropriate actions can be taken. This is the key goal of business activity monitoring (BAM). The result is the management of business events. To measure the appropriate processes or subprocesses, such controlling systems are configured on the basis of the aforementioned process models. They allow the "measurement" of the success of a process innovation and provide the information necessary for "smart" decisions.

The most important aspect of a functional open BPM environment is the integration between process design, implementation, and the following execution. The use of standards in this field enables the integration of process execution solutions (mainly SOA platforms) from various vendors (e.g., those necessary to support mergers and acquisitions when the merging organizations have different execution platforms in place). This can be done without the high costs of development and maintenance for software interfaces.

The consequent use of standards within open BPM also supports the management of processes across organizations, resulting in the collaboration of enterprises [18]. Therefore, collaboration innovation is well supported through this approach. This can, e.g., lead to a new more flexible supply chain process. Interactive Web-based applications, as offered by the "Web 2.0" [6] movement, can be integrated

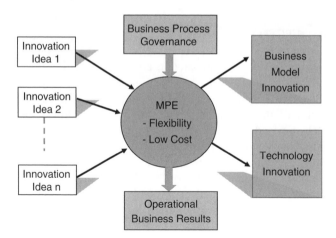

Fig. 2.9 MPE – enabler of innovation

with business processes and support a collaboration environment within and across the organization effectively.

The agility delivered by MPE enables innovation, especially business process innovation. Directed by the guidelines defined in a "business process governance approach," which will be discussed later, MPE facilitates the delivery of desired business results, especially process innovation, defined in process models. Innovation ideas can be evaluated through the flexibility to test new processes in a simulation or prototype mode and measure the results. Then, an enterprise can decide whether an innovation idea should be implemented and rolled out in the form of business model or technology innovation, mainly delivered through the necessary business process innovation. This effect is illustrated in Fig. 2.9.

Although MPE provides the necessary infrastructure, there are still entrepreneurial tasks left to define the innovation content that is evaluated and implemented. Market, technology, and process developments must be monitored to define which innovation areas should be addressed. For example, a structured, formalized market and product description can be very helpful. MPE facilitates but cannot automatically produce innovation.

The structured design of business processes is a good starting point in process innovation with MPE. One example is a North American producer of commodity chemicals, such as plastic foils. Differentiation through products is nearly impossible. Process innovation is extremely important. Therefore, the company defined process innovation as a key corporate initiative. Every business unit manager delivers suggestions for process innovation in the form of process models, so that an evaluation and potential implementation can be carried out easily.

Siemens and Intel, both high-tech enterprises, similarly facilitated the innovation of their mutual supply chain management (SCM). The intercompany collaboration processes were defined on the basis of the SCOR standard delivered by the Supply Chain Council [11]. Innovations included in the supply chain structure enabled an

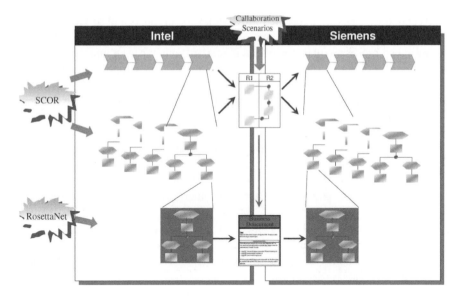

Fig. 2.10 Intel-Siemens: SCM innovation

efficient roll out of changes and standards across the organizations. Their approach is visualized in Fig. 2.10.

Mitsui, a leading Japanese trading company, has followed a similar innovation facilitation. As a service company, process innovation is basically the only effective form of innovation. Mitsui can also use its existing BPM environment to transfer innovation ideas from one location to another or to measure the effects of such initiatives.

Business Process Innovation has also found its way into the educational and academic practice. Universities, such as Widener University in Philadelphia, Pennsylvania, offer certifications and master's degree programs with a focus on business process innovation [19]. This allows enterprises to recruit employees who are familiar with innovation management in a process environment and can help put process innovation through MPE in practice.

2.4 The Bottom Line

The key messages of this chapter include the following:

- The main types of innovation are business model and technology innovation (Sect. 2.1).
- Business model innovation includes new or modified value propositions, new business processes (especially in the supply chain), or new target customers and markets (Sect. 2.1).

- Technology innovation has the following levers: products and services, process technologies, and enabling technologies (Sect. 2.1).
- Business processes play an essential role in both types of innovation; thus, business process innovation plays a pivotal role in all innovation initiatives (Sect. 2.1).
- Some companies are completely based on the notion of business process innovation (Sect. 2.1).
- To help ensure long-term business success and high performance, innovation must be part of daily business and an innovation process has to be put in place (Sect. 2.2).
- The innovation process defines the areas of innovation, the development of innovation ideas, and the realization of innovations, based on those ideas (Sect. 2.2).
- External partners should be included in the innovation process (Sect. 2.2).
- Through the use of business and technology standards, MPE ensures maximum flexibility at minimum cost, thus ensuring the necessary agility for business process innovation (Sect. 2.3).
- The most important aspect of a functional open BPM environment within MPE is the integration among process design, implementation, and the follow-on execution. This delivers the ability to progress quickly from design to execution in the case of change (Sect. 2.3).

References

1. Fingar, P: Extreme Competition – Innovation and the Great 21st Century Business Reformation. Meghan-Kiffer, Tampa (2006)
2. Kirchmer, M: Process innovation through open BPM. In: Pantaleo, D, Pal, N (eds.) From Strategy to Execution – Turning Accelerated Global Change into Opportunity, pp. 87–105. Springer, Berlin (2008)
3. Davila, T, Epstein, M J, Shelton, R: Making Innovation Work. Wharton School Publishing, Upper Saddle River (2006)
4. Christensen, C., Johnson, M.: Business model innovation. Report to the US Council of Innovation, The Conference Board (2007)
5. Christensen, C M, Raymour, M: The Innovator's Solution: Using Good Theory to Solve the Dilemmas of Growth. Harvard Business School Press, Boston (2003)
6. Wikipedia (ed.): Web 2.0. In: wikipedia.org (2007)
7. George, M, Works, J, Watson-Hemphill, K: Fast Innovation – Achieving Superior Differentiation, Speed to Market, and Increased Profitability. McGraw-Hill, New York (2005)
8. Johnson, M., Suskewicz, J.: Accelerating innovation. In: Pantaleo, D., Pal, N. (eds.): From Strategy to Execution – Turning Accelerated Global Change into Opportunity, pp. 49–64. Berlin (2008)
9. Hammer, M.: Six steps to operational innovation. In: Harvard Business School Working Knowledge for Business. hbswk.hbs.edu (2005). Accessed 30 Aug 2005
10. Bartlett, C A, Ghoshal, S: Managing Across Boraders – The Transnational Solution. Harvard Business School Press, Boston (2002)

11. Kirchmer, M, Brown, G, Heinzel, H: Using SCOR and other reference models for e-business process networks. In: Scheer, A-W, Abolhassan, E, Jost, W, Kirchmer, M (eds.) Business Process Excellence – ARIS in Practice, pp. 45–64. Springer, Berlin (2002)
12. IDS Scheer A.G. (ed.): ARIS design platform – ARIS enterprise architecture solution. White Paper. Saarbruecken (2006)
13. Scheer, A-W: ARIS – Business Process Modeling, 2nd edn. Springer, Berlin (1998)
14. Woods, D: Enterprise Service Architectures. O'Reilly, Beijing/Cambridge/Koeln, and others (2003)
15. Scheer, A W, Abolhassan, F, Jost, W, Kirchmer, M (eds.): Business Process Automation – ARIS in Practice. Springer, Berlin (2004)
16. Wikipedia (ed.): Business Process Execution Language. In: wikipedia.org (2007)
17. Hess, H., Blickle, T.: From process efficiency to organizational performance. ARIS Platform Expert Paper. Saarbruecken (2007)
18. Kirchmer, M.: E-business process networks – successful value chains through standards. J. Enterprise. Manage. **17**(1) (2004)
19. Widener University, School for Business Administration: Business Process Innovation. At: www.widener.edu (2007)

Chapter 3
Information Technology Enabling Process Execution with MPE

Most business processes within an organization are at least partially supported by IT. Enterprise resource planning (ERP), customer relationship management (CRM), supply chain management (SCM), or similar systems are present in one or the other way in almost every enterprise. Many executives are already considering new IT architectures on the basis of SOA or are in the midst of such an implementation. Some companies even take these ideas to the next level, such as those working toward the use of Web 2.0 applications. But what does it all mean? How do these IT components fit into management of process excellence (MPE)?

The entire process of MPE is supported by application software systems, often referred to as "BPM tools." Until now, we have primarily discussed about support of the design phase and the transition to the implementation activities through modeling and related software. However, most private and public organizations consider BPM in relation to the aforementioned operational systems. These systems are software environments that support the execution of processes and, therefore, are relevant for the implementation and execution phase of MPE.

I had been working for over 10 years in the field of ERP implementations and have written many publications about the experiences during those projects of "process-oriented implementations" [1]. In the last years, however, I focused on new software architectures, based on service-oriented architecture (SOA) and moving toward the use of the Web and its new capabilities [2, 3]. In both the areas, I have practical experience and conducted a fair amount of research. In this chapter, I share my thoughts regarding the developments of IT to support business processes.

This chapter will explore important process execution environments and their relation to MPE. Major topics include ERP, SOA, and the Web 2.0-based "Enterprise 2.0," all which influence all phases of MPE. Their successful deployment is a crucial factor for the successful application of MPE. The IT orientation discussed in this chapter is shown in Fig. 3.1.

However, it is important to remember that MPE is not just about technology, as previously explained. On the one hand, IT is a key enabler, but without other components, especially the people involved, the approach will not work. On the other hand, without enabling technology, many MPE activities would just be

M. Kirchmer, *High Performance Through Process Excellence*,
DOI 10.1007/978-3-642-21165-2_3, © Springer-Verlag Berlin Heidelberg 2011

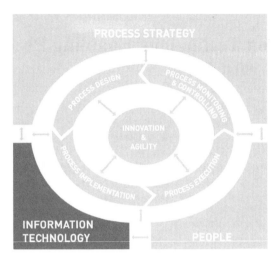

Fig. 3.1 Focus on information technology of MPE

theories, as BPM was during its early days. Although I agree with the "concept of replacing chief information officers" (CIOs) with "chief process officers" (CPOs) [4, 5], it would be essential also for the CPO to have a strong understanding of IT and its enabling power for achieving business processes that enable high performance for the organization as a whole.

3.1 ERP: The "Traditional" Path to Process Execution

During the last 10–15 years, an increasing number of business processes have been supported by standard software packages, such as ERP, SCM, or CRM systems [1, 6]. The most popular are ERP systems, covering the majority of a company's operational activities, such as sales, material management, production planning and control, maintenance, asset management, finance, financial controlling, human resources, etc. In this chapter, ERP will be used as the primary example for such standard software applications. Major vendors include SAP [7], Oracle [8], and Microsoft [9]. The use of standard software has numerous advantages when compared with individually developed software systems, including:

- Lower cost of procurement
- Faster procurement, time savings
- Smoother migration of the organization during the software implementation because of best practices in implementation approaches
- Lower maintenance cost
- Reduction or elimination of application development backlogs, focus of development on company specifics
- Protection of the investment through continuous support by vendor and large user community

- Delivers necessary functionality and data integration, which enables the support of processes
- Business skills of the software vendor and the other users
- Often a higher ergonomic and technology standard

Although there are also some disadvantages, like dependence on a software vendor or lengthy implementations, the advantages described above are generally considered to outweigh the disadvantages by far. Most organizations use standard application software wherever possible and develop custom software only for the areas not covered by those systems.

Standard software systems for operational business applications, especially ERP systems, offer the following key benefits [6]:

- Reduction in cycle times
- Faster information transactions
- More accurate financial management
- Creation of the basis for e-business, inter-enterprise processes
- Visibility of hidden process knowledge

A key advantage of these "traditional" standard software solutions is that they not only deliver technology to execute a specific process, but also provide best business practices. The software reflects its vendor's business knowledge regarding a certain topic or industry, as well as the experience of the vendor with other customers in the same area.

The successful use of standard software, such as ERP systems, implies the design and execution of business processes, according to the delivered best practices of the software solution. If you buy an ERP system, you do not just purchase a piece of technology; you also buy a set of predefined business processes. In turn, you have to adapt at least part of your organization to the requirements of the software-based business processes. For example, you may be forced to create some material master data before you send out a procurement order. ERP systems include a process definition that is more or less coded in the software. The software only allows very limited changes or adjustments of its process definition. These adjustments can be done during the software configuration through the setting of specific parameters. This is a key task of ERP implementation activities.

Modifications to the delivered process logic often result in modification to software that lead, in most cases, to tremendous cost. I have seen companies with departments of more than 30 people solely focused on transferring ERP system modifications from one release to the other. Many of the advantages of standard software are lost if you decide to modify that software. However, most of the standard systems allow the integration of "add-on software" through predefined interfaces. But this is, in many cases, insufficient, especially for the support of a process that is critical to achieving competitive advantage. As a result, new business processes are not adequately supported by traditional software solutions, which negatively impacts productivity and performance.

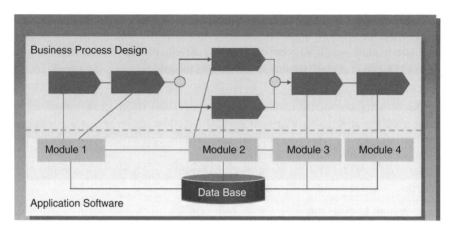

Fig. 3.2 Standard software (e.g., ERP): integration of process design and technology

The process definitions delivered through standard software are more and more often described in so-called "software reference models," which document the best practices supported by the application system (we will discuss reference models in more detail later). "Next business practices," or process designs that are only starting to emerge in an industry, are generally not supported [2, 3]. This is because they require new processes that were not considered during the standard software development. Only when a next practice eventually becomes a best practice, it will be included in the traditional standard software solution.

The tight integration of the business process definition and software technology in traditional standard software systems is visualized in Fig. 3.2.

Although standard software systems, such as ERP systems, can be used to support business processes, the software is still developed in a function-oriented way. It consists of modules that reflect certain business functions, such as a sales module, a shipping module, or a production planning module. There are generally no process modules, such as an "order-to-delivery" module for the "consumer packaged goods industry." Such a process would require the implementation of several modules to be supported properly.

Consequently, the business process support through ERP systems must be accomplished during the implementation. Therefore, MPE requires a business process-oriented implementation approach for function-oriented developed ERP, SCM, CRM, or similar standard software systems. This means that during the implementation of the software into the enterprise, all modules necessary to support an entire business process have to be implemented.

For example, a company producing industry compressors has identified three core business processes. The "engineer-to-order" processes cover all activities from the customer-order processing, engineering, and production to distribution. The processes are generally optimized on the basis of quality aspects. A customer would be willing to wait days, or even weeks, longer for an engineered-to-order compressor, but it must have the highest quality once it is in the factory. A second process is focused on "make-to-order" compressors, smaller machines that are produced based on customer order, but according to standard specifications. The process does not require engineering activities. It is optimized under cost considerations because competitors build similar products – but for a higher price. The third process is focused on "customer service." It basically supports the distribution of spare parts from stock. Customers in need of spare parts are usually under great time pressure. Therefore, the process has to be optimized under cycle time aspects.

If an ERP system were implemented according to the software structure, all similar activities of the three processes would be treated the same. No specific configuration, just focus on the goals of one of the three processes, would take place. The initially process-oriented designed organizations would be replaced by the functional structure of the software. This can be avoided by a process-oriented implementation approach, as suggested by MPE [1, 6]. It ensures the support of each process through properly configured standard software modules. This approach to the implementation phase is shown in Fig. 3.3. This means that the business process design (reflecting the capabilities of the ERP or similar standard software system) is used to drive the configuration of the standard software package. The process models can then be used to test and verify the software configuration. This is visualized in Fig. 3.4.

This approach works well, as long as the organization is satisfied with the best practices offered by the standard software, using the predefined adjustments during the configuration. Experience and recent Accenture research has shown that this works for 80–85% of all business processes. Why should one consider the

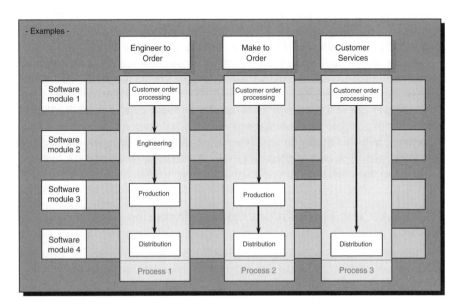

Fig. 3.3 Process-oriented implementation of function-oriented software (e.g., ERP)

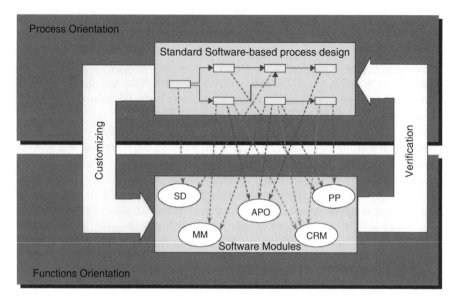

Fig. 3.4 Business process-driven standard software configuration

company-specific organization of financial processes that are highly regulated through legal requirements? Also, processes such as human resources administration, procurement of standard materials, etc., are typically not critical to achieve competitive advantage. Therefore, a best-practice solution is the most appropriate.

The standard application software can also be hosted by a third-party company, an application service provider (ASP). This allows an enterprise to just focus on the business aspects of the software and outsource the technical topics. The pricing for the use can even be adjusted to the demand of the specific enterprise.

But how should one handle the 15–20% of the business processes that we want to implement and execute on the basis of a unique company-specific design, the processes that are truly important to provide competitive advantage? These processes deliver the real competitive advantage, but also require more flexible IT support. Until now, the only solution was an individual software development from the scratch, followed by the difficult integration and maintenance issues caused by the ERP system. The next-generation process automation, based on SOA, delivers a solution to that challenge. Let us discuss how that works.

3.2 SOA: New Flexibility in Process Execution

Key processes tend to be strongly influenced by a company's specific offerings (products or services) and the related market demands, so standard software applications like ERP cannot deliver the required best possible IT support because they reflect the needs of wider user communities. SOAs offer a solution for those needs. They enable separation of the business process design and support through appropriate software applications or application components delivered as so-called services (we will use "service" as synonym for an application software component, delivering specific results needed to support one or several functions of a business process). This means that application software can be used exactly as required by business processes. SOA provides the environment to link the required application components and exchange data as necessary to support the overlying business processes design [2, 10–12]. This enables the execution of next-practice business processes, that of business-process innovation. In other words, it is IT for business-process innovation, as Woods and Mattern, some of the first authors of a book about SOA, describe SOA [12] – a perfect fit to support the goals of agility and innovation of MPE.

The use of SOA can lead to significant reductions in IT maintenance costs because expensive program-to-program interfaces of traditional software environments are avoided. All software components are simply linked into the integration environment of the SOA [12]. This resolves many of the issues of extending ERP systems through add-on applications supporting enterprise-specific processes or subprocesses.

These integration capabilities are also the basis for the reuse of software components in the case of custom developments, thus resulting in cost savings. Once a software component or service is developed, it can be used to support several processes. It can be part of another integrated process-oriented software system.

The true value of SOA, however, is only delivered when the environment is used to support business change, to enable agility and process innovation. The process design can be improved and cost and time efficiently implemented, through the selection and adjustment of the application components needed to support the specific processes. New "services" can be added, and others deleted or modified, according to the requirements of the business processes. The same procedure can be used to realize completely new or strongly modified processes, thus enabling business process innovation. SOA can be used to support the fast execution of process designs, reflecting strategic directions. Thus, SOA plays a critical role of transferring strategy into operational performance through MPE. It enables the execution of the strategic direction. These effects are illustrated in Fig. 3.5.

If SOA is utilized solely to reduce IT costs, the greatest value of the new software architecture is missed. SOA only delivers actual strategic impact when it is used to drive innovation and agility in an organization. It must become the compelling force behind business-process improvement and process-innovation initiatives.

Therefore, the knowledge about new or modified processes needs to be transferred efficiently and effectively into the technical components of SOA. This makes SOA a key component of MPE.

To understand and apply this tight but flexible integration between process design, implementation, and execution, a more detailed analysis of SOA and its components is necessary. The core of SOA is middleware that separates the process-design information in the form of process models from the executing software services. This middleware consists of a workflow component that allows the definition of the specific process logic and an integration component calling the

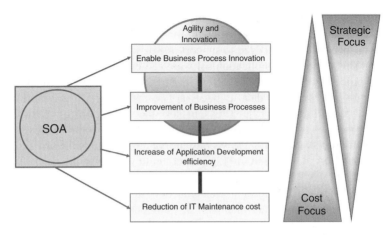

Fig. 3.5 Business impacts of SOA

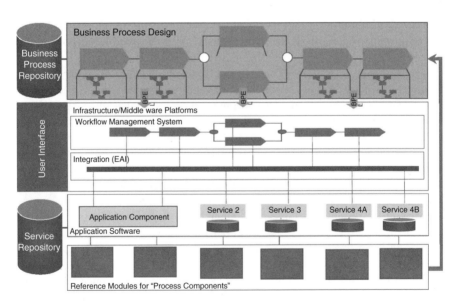

Fig. 3.6 Service-oriented architecture (SOA)

right software services for each function of the defined work flow. The work flow is defined on the basis of the process models developed in the process-design phase. This design is supported through reference models, describing the subprocesses executed through a specific existing service. SOA also delivers one consistent user interface, independent of the various software services used to support a process. The concept of SOA is shown in Fig. 3.6.

The most important aspect of SOA is the integration of process design and execution. During the design phase, business-process knowledge is created in the form of process models, which describe the blueprint of the enterprise. They contain all business-process knowledge necessary to implement and execute those processes. This business-process knowledge must be transferred to the execution layer of SOA, enabling IT-supported process execution.

Although IT support for business-process design (through modeling tools) can be optimized for the development and description of successful business aspects (as explained during the discussion of the process factory), the technical SOA components are constructed to ensure an efficient and effective technical execution of the designed processes. The middleware brings everything together.

The separation of application software technology and process design enables business-driven IT, providing the flexibility necessary for continuous process improvement and innovation – thus resulting in business agility.

Services (or applications) can be stored within an enterprise or at a third-party IT environment. In the latter case, they are procured through the Web, and thus are called Web services. This makes an enterprise independent from technical changes and new IT developments. A company can focus on the application of IT to support the business processes.

SOA can be built, based on software products, such as SAP NetWeaver [13], Oracle Fusion [14], Microsoft BizTalk [15], IBM Websphere [16], or many others. The first three mentioned vendors also deliver traditional standard software. They decided to move toward a next-generation SOA software architecture to deliver more flexible process-oriented solutions. In other words, they offer the described middleware platforms, but also some of the required services (components of their standard software packages or completely new developed software, reflecting their business expertise in new software technology). However, SOA also opens the doors for new, smaller software companies that may just deliver some very specialized services used in a larger vendor's SOA environment. Some examples of smaller vendors of SOA-based environments include Global 360 [17] and Pegasystems [18]. Another example is jCOMl, which delivers an integrated environment for fast realization of simple SOA-based business processes [19].

The integration of the design software (modeling tool) supporting the MPE process factory and the SOA environment is extremely important for MPE. For example, the aforementioned ARIS Platform is integrated with all of the aforementioned SOA environments and even several more [20]. When selecting a software application for the business process factory, this integration aspect should be an important selection criterium.

SOA allows the combination of existing applications with new applications, avoiding or at least reducing integration challenges experienced in traditional application environments. This enables the integration of best and next practices. However, to automate next practices or other very company-specific business processes, one may not even need new application functionality. It may be sufficient to use existing application functionality (e.g., from an ERP or SCM application) in a new process logic. SOA environments allow the rapid development of such "composite applications" [21]. These composite applications deliver a process definition, an appropriately configured workflow and data integration. They use one or several existing software modules. Composite applications support a specific "new" business process, which has not been supported by the existing software solution.

These composite applications are built on existing standard software and can be offered as packaged solutions on the software market, a way of distributing new business practices [21]. Software or consulting companies, or even end-use companies, may develop such composite applications. For example, packaged composite applications are delivered by SAP and some of its partners [22].

Many enterprises utilize not one SOA environment, but various SOA products from multiple vendors or even self-developed platform software. Some possible reasons for such utilization include mergers and acquisitions, different strategies in divisions of an enterprise group, or other historic developments in a company or enterprise group. The use of multiple platforms generally still allows an enterprise to achieve the described benefits of SOA. For example, each platform can support one or several business processes. Or the platforms can be integrated using their own integration technology so that one process can be supported through multiple platforms. However, it is important that the process models, the knowledge about business process, are stored in the process warehouse of the process factory for distribution to the various SOA environments. This is the precondition for an effective enterprise-wide process management as required by MPE. The use of multiple SOA environments driven through one process factory is visualized in Fig. 3.7. This is another application of the "open BPM" principles explained earlier.

SOA delivers a new dimension of flexibility, supporting the goals of MPE. However, this flexibility does not come without a price. It requires a thorough process design, resulting in semantically and syntactically correct process models. These models are necessary to manage the available flexibility. That is why,

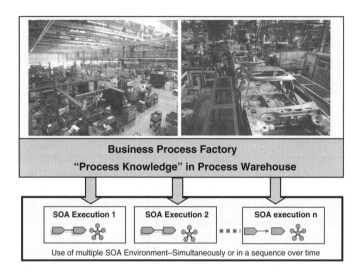

Fig. 3.7 Process factory with multiple SOA environments

a functioning process factory within MPE is essential for the use of SOA. Because 70% or more of an organization's processes are often irrelevant for achieving competitive advantage or any form of process innovation, the use of traditional standard software is still appealing for those areas. For many enterprises, the combination of ERP and similar systems with SOA may be the best solution for process execution.

SOA also allows integration with other companies' software applications, especially via the Web. Therefore, it is also an enabler of inter-enterprise processes, like those presented in the Intel-Siemens case in Chap. 2. Such processes across several organizations are key enablers of high-performance enterprises [5].

The Web and its application play a pivotal role. New, interactive Web applications lead to a new business environment guided through MPE. We will now discuss the IT architecture of the next-generation enterprise.

3.3 Enterprise 2.0+: The Next Generation of Process Execution

New IT architectures are clearly driven by the World Wide Web (WWW). The common opinion that the Internet hype would end after the burst of the dot-com bubble in 2001 has been proven wrong. On the contrary, Web capabilities have continuously improved and the ability to bring people and organizations together in communities has become more important than ever [5]. The new generation of WWW capabilities is often called "Web 2.0."

Web 2.0 can be perceived as the second generation of Web-based communities and hosted services, which aim to facilitate creativity, collaboration, and the sharing of ideas and data between users. The term was created and promoted in a conference organized by O'Reilly Media in 2004 [23]. O'Reilly characterized Web 2.0 by describing the core competencies of Web 2.0 companies [24] as follows:

- Instead of packaged software, services (procured through the web) with cost-effective scalability are used
- Control over unique, hard-to-recreate data sources, which get richer as more and more people use these sources
- Trusting users as codevelopers
- Harnessing collective intelligence
- Customer self-service
- Software above the level of single devices
- Lightweight user interfaces, development models, and business models

A key differentiator of any Web 2.0 service or application continuously improves the results and usefulness as more people utilize it. Therefore, such an application either solicits data directly from the user or finds intelligent data-mining capabilities to continuously produce better data. Those Web pages are called "wikis." Examples of such Web 2.0 applications include the online encyclopedia Wikipedia, created and maintained by its users; social networks, like "LinkedIn"; and Google Search, which improves search results, based on characteristics of past searches [24, 25]. Web 2.0 applications often utilize so-called "mashups," composite applications using data or functionality from existing Web applications and combining them with new content, delivering additional value to the user without changing the original sources [26]. An example is HousingMaps.com, which combines mapping functionality from "Google Maps" with apartment rental information [26].

Some people are already talking about Web 3.0, which combines the capabilities of Web 2.0 with the so-called "Semantic Web" [27]. This brings structure to the data masses and enables users to find desired information more efficiently. On the basis of this structure, it will be easier to find the information needed and to make ready use of all the data available through the Web. This is another step forward in the development of the WWW.

Although the aforementioned Web 2.0 applications are more focused on private users, there are already many current initiatives to transfer those capabilities into the business world, targeting enterprise clients. The result is the "Enterprise 2.0." Enterprise 2.0 is a company using the capabilities of Web 2.0 for its business purposes, including a "business-to-business" (B2B) environment [25, 28]. In this context, the term "Management 2.0" is used to express the idea that these new Web capabilities require an appropriate management approach [29]. In this book, we discuss the Enterprise 2.0"+" to reflect that future Web developments can also be included in the overall architecture.

Enterprise 2.0+ technologies encompass the following six components [30]:

- Search capabilities: They enable users to easily find the information for which they are looking
- Links: The information about links between Web pages is utilized
- Authoring: Users author content of Web pages (e.g., in the form of blogs)
- Tags: Users categorize information through tags to make it more accessible
- Extensions: Applications automate a part of the categorization work by suggesting content to users, based on past clicks
- Signals: Users are informed when new content of interest is published

A look at the IT architecture inside the Enterprise 2.0+ is shown in Fig. 3.8. The core is an SOA environment integrated with one BPM engine for design and implementation and another integrated component for the management and control of the executed business processes [31]. On the basis of SOA, some processes are triggered by specific external events, resulting in an event-driven SOA. This real-time event management is also reflected in the BPM software.

Quality issues in delivered materials may immediately trigger quality assurance processes, or the arrival of a specific customer-order type may lead to certain order-handling activities. Extraordinary events, such as extreme cycle times for an order, may lead to correcting activities related to the specific process instance. This generally leads to a near real-time reaction to various events initiating and acting on process instances (that means how, e.g., a specific customer-order XYZ is handled in a process) instead of a focus on a more general process design, applied

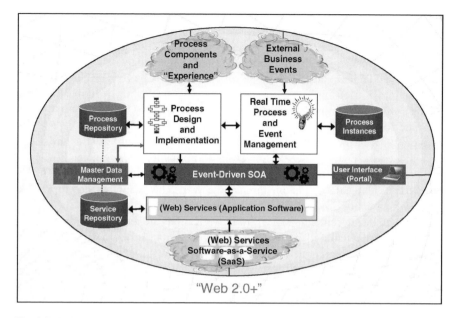

Fig. 3.8 Inside the Enterprise 2.0+

to many process instances. The master data management (MDM) is handled across all processes to avoid redundancies and inconsistencies.

The BPM design component can receive external input through the Web. This may include general experiences regarding certain business issues or formal reference models showing relevant business practices. In return, an enterprise also provides this information to others. The BPM event management also reacts to external events, such as price changes for raw materials, or general macroeconomic events, like changes and trends of currency exchange rates. The SOA may not only use internal software components, but may also support business processes though application services delivered via the Web, the aforementioned Web services. These services can even be rented. You just pay for the "service" of getting the software provided as you need the service. This concept is called software-as-a-service (SaaS) – promoted by Web 2.0. In general, the use of IT capabilities through the Internet is more and more referred to as cloud computing.

These approaches lead to the fact that the Enterprise 2.0+ is highly integrated with the business environment, as shown in Fig. 3.9. A company may be member of many online communities. Imagine using an environment like Youtube to exchange business process models. Instead of posting videos, companies could post process models representing their organization's best business practices or other interesting process ideas. This could facilitate the exchange of business experiences within and across specific industries.

The Web 2.0 environment could be utilized to make the Enterprise 2.0+ part of a powerful virtual organization. For example, one could create an innovation network

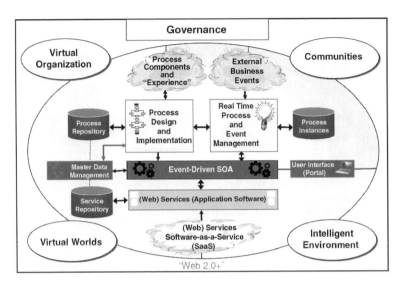

Fig. 3.9 Enterprise 2.0+: integrated with business environment

around the company, including customers, partners, research institutes, universities, etc. The exchange of ideas could be organized through blogs (derived from "Web log"). A blog is a Web site where entries are written in chronological order and generally displayed in reverse chronological order [32]. Members of the network make their entries and the blog facilitator includes them in the overall innovation process.

Until now, most information systems received necessary data through human interaction. For example, a person enters the shipping data of orders. This is often very costly and leads to delays. New technologies, like radio frequency identification (RFID), enable the automated creation of that data. For example, once containers are loaded into a ship, this information is automatically transferred through RFID into a software system and from there becomes available through the Web. The result is an "intelligent environment" or the "Internet of things" [33, 34], which ultimately leads to business processes that enable high performance. But similar technologies can also be used to improve products and services, leading to "intelligent products" that behave in a context-sensitive way [33]. An example is cars automatically moving toward a destination and breaking whenever necessary.

This intelligent environment closes the gap between the real and the virtual world step by step. Once you have more and more information about the real-world digitized, you can start using this information as building blocks for a virtual world, allowing the realistic test of new business process as described earlier. And, the boundaries between the real and virtual worlds then begin to blur.

A key challenge of Enterprise 2.0+ is finding the appropriate governance model. Web 2.0 empowers people and encourages creativity. But how do you ensure that they still work toward the company's goals? A traditional governance model, consisting of many inflexible rules and policies, does not work in such an environment.

The Enterprise 2.0+ could utilize a governance model similar to that of the online encyclopedia Wikipedia. Users are guided through common goals and control themselves. However, it is clear that an enterprise is more complex, so the governance has to be more refined. But the direction is demonstrated by Web 2.0 communities like Wikipedia. We will discuss the topic business process governance in more detail later.

The Enterprise 2.0+ is clearly a perfect environment for MPE. It permanently delivers the information necessary for timely decisions and supports the almost real-time execution of the resulting actions. Strategy and operational performance are closely integrated. Agility and innovation are strongly encouraged.

But the Enterprise 2.0+ also demonstrates that ultimately, high performance depends on people and the way they act within their business processes. They have to feel comfortable with and accept the upcoming change. In the next chapter, we will discuss how this change can be managed.

3.4 Bottom Line

- Traditional standard software solutions, like ERP systems, not only deliver a technology to execute a specific process, but also best business practices (Sect. 3.1).
- The use of ERP and similar standard software systems means you must somewhat adapt your organization to the requirements of the software-based business processes. This works well for most of the processes, but creates challenges for the processes necessary to create competitive advantage because they are company specific (Sect. 3.1).
- A business process-oriented implementation approach is required for function-oriented developed ERP or similar software systems. In other words, during the implementation of the software into the enterprise, all modules necessary to support an entire business process must be implemented. Otherwise, the implementation leads back to a functional organization (Sect. 3.1).
- SOA enables the separation of the business process design and support through appropriate application software components. Consequently, the application software can be used exactly as required by the company-specific business processes (Sect. 3.2).
- The true value of SOA is only delivered when the environment is used to support business change, to enable agility and process innovation (Sect. 3.2).
- The knowledge about new or modified processes can be transferred efficiently and effectively into the technical components of SOA, based on a tight integration of process design software (modeling software) and the SOA execution environment (Sect. 3.2).
- SOA delivers a new dimension of flexibility; however, this flexibility does not come without a price. It requires a thorough process design, resulting in semantically and syntactically correct process models (Sect. 3.2).

- Web 2.0 can be perceived as the second generation of Web-based communities and hosted services, which facilitate creativity, collaboration, and sharing of ideas and data between users. The use of Web 2.0 and related concepts in a business environment leads to the Enterprise 2.0+ (Sect. 3.3).
- The Enterprise 2.0+ is highly integrated with the business environment, participating in communities, acting as part of virtual organizations, and using technologies to digitize the real environment to make it a component of virtual worlds (Sect. 3.3).
- A key challenge of the Enterprise 2.0+ is to find the appropriate governance model (Sect. 3.3).

References

1. Kirchmer, M: Business Process Oriented Implementation of Standard Software – How to Achieve Competitive Advantage Efficiently and Effectively, 2nd edn. Springer, Berlin (1999)
2. Kirchmer, M, Scheer, A W: Business process automation – combining best and next practices. In: Scheer, A W, Abolhassan, E, Jost, W, Kirchmer, M (eds.) Business Process Automation – ARIS in Practice, pp. 1–15. Springer, Berlin (2004)
3. Kirchmer, M.: Knowledge communication empowers SOA for business agility. In: Proceedings of the 11th World Multi-conference on Systemics, Cybernetics and Informatics, July 8–11, 2007, vol. 3, pp. 301–307. Orlando (2007)
4. Jost, W.: Vom CIO zum CPO. In: Harvard Business Manager (2004)
5. Fingar, P: Extreme Competition – Innovation and the Great 21st Century Business Reformation. Meghan-Kiffer, Tampa (2006)
6. Davenport, T: Mission Critical – Realizing the Promise of Enterprise Systems. Harvard Business School, Boston (2000)
7. SAP AG (ed.): http://wwwll.sap.com/usa/solutions/business-suite/erp/index.epx (2007)
8. Oracle, Inc. (ed.): http://www.oracle.com/apphcations/e-business-suite.html (2007)
9. Microsoft, Inc. (ed.): http://www.microsoft.com/dynamics/default.mspx (2007)
10. Woods, D: Enterprise Service Architectures. O'Reilly, Beijing (2003)
11. Kalakota, R, Robinson, M: Service Blueprint: A Roadmap for Execution. Addison-Wesley, Boston (2003)
12. Woods, D, Mattern, T: Enterprise SOA – Designing IT for Business Innovation. O'Reilly, Bejing (2006)
13. SAP AG (ed.): SAP NetWeaver helps put you ahead of the curve. In: sap.com (2007)
14. Oracle, Inc. (ed.): Oracle fusion – next generation applications. In: oracle.com (2007)
15. Microsoft, Inc. (ed.): Your business – connected. BizTalk. In: Microsoft.com (2007)
16. Newman, D.: BPM & SOA: Real world stories of business success. In: IQPC (ed.): Proceedings of the Business Process Management Summit, Las Vegas (2007)
17. www.global360.com (2007)
18. www.pega.com (2007)
19. Fleischmann, A.: Subject-oriented Business Process Management. White Paper, Muenchen, June 2007
20. IDS Scheer AG (ed.): ARIS Platform. Product Brochure. Saarbruecken (2007)
21. Woods, D: Packaged Composite Applications. O'Reilly, Beijing (2003)
22. Stolz, H.: Composite applications framework – designing cross solutions. In: SAP AG (ed.): SAP Info – Quick Guide: SAP NetWeaver – The Power of Lower TCO, p. 40. (2003)
23. Wikipedia. (ed): Web 2.0. In: www.wikipedia.com (2007)

24. O'Reilly, T.: What is web 2.0 – design patterns and business models for the next generation of software. In: www.oreilly.com (2005)
25. Heuser, L., Alsdorf, G, Woods, D.: International Research Forum 2006 – Web 2.0 – IT Security-Real World Awareness – IT as a Tool for Growth and Development. New York (2006)
26. Bradly, A., Gootzit, D.: Who's who in enterprise 'Mashup' technologies. In: Gartner Research, ID Number: G00151351 (2007)
27. Wahlster, W, Dengel, A.: Web 3.0 convergence of web 2.0 and the semantic web. In: Technology Radar Feature Paper, Edition 11/2006, Germany (2006)
28. Heuser, L., Alsdorf, C, Woods, D.: Enterprise 2.0, The Service Grid, User-Driven Innovation, Business Model Transformation – International Research Forum 2007. New York (2008)
29. Lochmaier, L.: Management 2.0 und der intelligente Schwarm. In: manager-magazin.de (2007)
30. McAffee, A.: Enterprise 2.0: the dawn of emergent collaboration. In: MIT Sloan Management Review, vol. 43, No. 3, Spring, (2006)
31. Carter, S: The New Language of Business – SOA & Web 2.0. IBM Press, Upper Saddle River/ Boston (2007)
32. Wikipedia. (ed): Blog. In: www.wikipedia.com 12/2007.
33. Fleisch, E, Christ, O, Dierkes, M: Die betriebswirtschafthche vision des internets der dinge. In: Fleisch, E, Mattern, F (eds.) Das Internet der Dinge – Ubiquitous Computing und RFID in der Praxis, pp. 3–37. Springer, Berlin (2005)
34. Matter, F: Die technische Basis fuer das Internet der Dinge. In: Fleisch, E., Mattern, F (ed.): Das Internet der Dinge – Ubiquitous Computing und RFID in der Praxis, pp. 39–66. Berlin (2005)

Chapter 4
Business Process Change Management for MPE

Change is a dominating factor in today's business environment. This is a key driver for applying business process-oriented management approaches in modern enterprises. New, flexible IT architectures like SOA support this change from a technology point-of-view, as we have discussed in the previous chapter. But how can you prepare people and help them cope with impending adjustments? People change management has become one of the greatest challenges for organizations if they are to achieve high performance. They have to cautiously manage their talent.

Looking at today's business world, there are various reasons for continuous change of business processes, such as the following examples [1]:

- New or changing customers, suppliers, or other market partners
- New or altered market offerings (goods, services, information, etc.)
- Changing legal regulations
- Availability of new or modified technologies, like IT applications
- Outsourcing processes or subprocesses
- Mergers and acquisitions
- New business models
- Cultural differences in new enterprise locations

All of the resulting changes affect one or several business processes. The execution of most of the processes requires a combination of people and technologies. Therefore, people change management is relevant for all. Even if a new technology is used to automate an entire process, this may result in change of processes for employees in the IT department. Again, change management is necessary.

In this chapter, we will discuss how to handle the people side of such process changes. People are the key process asset when using MPE. Consequently, we will discuss related topics in this chapter. This focus is shown in Fig. 4.1. People aspects are relevant for all phases of MPE, as shown in the life cycle model.

M. Kirchmer, *High Performance Through Process Excellence*,
DOI 10.1007/978-3-642-21165-2_4, © Springer-Verlag Berlin Heidelberg 2011

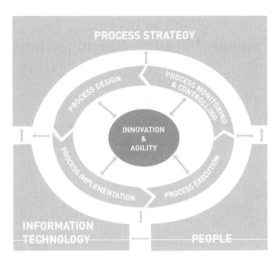

Fig. 4.1 Focus on people aspects of MPE

4.1 What Is Business Process Change Management?

Let us look at a few examples of business process change. The business-driven application of new technologies, like "mobile-business" (m-business), can result in many business process changes [2]. An example is shown in Fig. 4.2. In a traditional process, a truck with office supplies arrives at an office supply store. Then, the truck driver checks with the store clerk, who consults his IT system to find out which supplies are needed. The truck driver documents the necessary inventory changes and fills the store shelves. Then, the store clerk books the inventory adjustments for his shop. The m-business process improves this procedure. With his mobile device, the truck driver accesses the store application systems so he can do all bookings by himself.

The ways in which cultural differences can influence business processes is visualized in Fig. 4.3. In a process typical of Japanese environments, there is a high focus on quality. The quality-assurance activities are carried out twice: on the customer side and on the supplier side. The redundancy ensures the highest-quality standards and demonstrates the characteristic Japanese attention to details, although the process is not 100% efficient. If efficiency is the main goal, these redundancies are eliminated. Depending on business goals and the cultural environment, one of the processes may be changed to the other. This is a question global companies would have to answer (we will discuss the effects of globalization more in detail later on).

All the described changes require the related modifications of existing business processes or the creation of new ones, thus business process change management is necessary. To ensure that such a change is really effective for an organization, the following conditions should be fulfilled [3]:

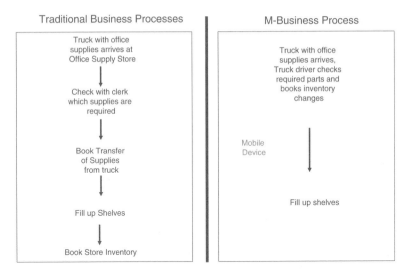

Fig. 4.2   M-business – technology drives business process changes

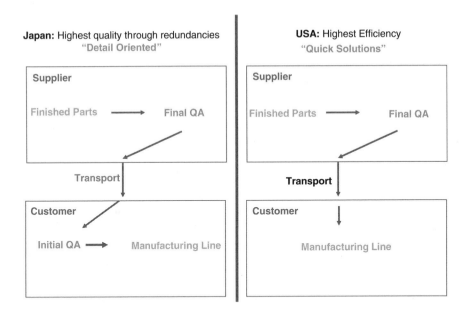

Fig. 4.3   Business processes can reflect cultural differences

- There must be a perceived advantage of the change that can be identified by the people who will have to make the change.
- The change must be compatible with the involved people's thought process.
- The change must be as easy-to-understand as possible.

- The change must be divisible and executable in phases or by different people.
- It must be possible to communicate the change clearly without using a new vocabulary with which people are not familiar.
- The change must be reversible and can be undone if things do not work out as expected.
- The change should be as cost efficient as possible and require as little time as possible from the people involved.
- The change has to treat people with respect; it must not result in embarrassment for the involved people.
- The initiator of the change must have credibility or a reputation of success.
- The change must be realistic and really do what it is supposed to do.
- The consequences of failure must be minimized.

In most business situations, it is not possible to fulfill all those requirements. However, experience has shown that at least seven to eight [3] of the requirements should be met in order to make a change truly successful. Change management then ensures the following conditions to the process change [4]:

- Necessary actions are initiated with an acceptable delay after the external change has occurred.
- Necessary actions are executed in a fast and effective way.
- All reactions and actions are initiated and executed in a controlled manner.

As explained, the effective management of the permanent change is a key success factor for an enterprise and a precondition to move from "good to great" [5]. It is of fundamental importance that the people involved in changing processes are able to understand and accept those changes, and ultimately, make them happen. Therefore, the most appropriate definition of change management includes the combination of the following activities [1, 6]:

- Information
- Communication
- Training

People must be informed of the changes and invited to provide feedback. An intense communication period typically occurs at this point. And finally, people have to be trained to be successful in the new business process environment. Figure 4.4 visualizes this basic definition for business process change management.

The content of the relevant information, communication, and training concerning specific business processes can be structured using the ARIS Architecture previously discussed [7, 8]. The major questions to be addressed in change management activities can be directly deducted from the ARIS information system views, as shown in Fig. 4.5:

- Who (people, departments, different enterprises, etc.) is involved in the change (organization view)?
- What are the new or modified functions and why are they better (function view)?
- What new or modified information is needed or produced and why is it better (data view)?

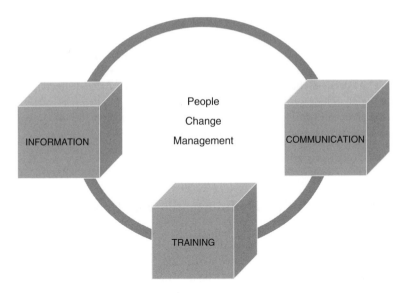

Fig. 4.4 Business process change management – the core activities

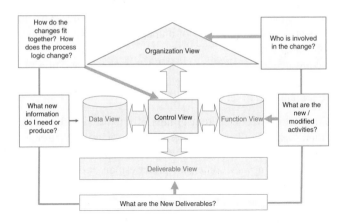

Fig. 4.5 Business process change management based on the ARIS architecture

- Which new or modified deliverables are expected and why (deliverable view)?
- How do the changes fit together and how do they influence and improve the overall process (control view)?

This structure for change management based on ARIS also ensures the overall integration into MPE because MPE also applies the ARIS framework and its principles to describe business processes. This leads to an overall consistent and integrated approach, which is necessary to ensure the required effectiveness of the approach. People-related activities are based on the same business process knowledge assets as IT-related activities.

Business process change management is again a process in and of itself. Information, communication, and training are subprocesses. Therefore, process-oriented methodologies and approaches (e.g., for the design or the implementation) can be applied to manage business process change. The principles of MPE can be used to organize the process change management. BPM software can be utilized to support change management within MPE [9].

We will now examine the elements of change management in more detail, starting with information and communication.

4.2 How Do You Provide Information and Communication?

The starting points of most change management activities are information and communication. Both must be adapted to the cultural environment of the enterprise and its specific situation. For example, you may need to act cautiously in a company that is in a bad economic situation because people may fear for their jobs. In a software enterprise founded only a few years ago, people may be more accustomed to change and accept it easily. In a 100-year-old, traditional manufacturing company, people may be much less accustomed to and less open to change. The situation in the public sector is also different because of numerous legal requirements and policies. Changing political situations?

The following general guidelines are related to the preparation of information and communication activities in an organization [6] starting a business process change management initiative:

- Segment the audience – Different groups of people must be addressed differently, in their "language" and considering their specific situation.
- Use multiple channels – People have personal preferences regarding where they like to get their news – some may prefer e-mail or other kinds of computer-based communication, while others are more open to phone or face-to-face communications.
- Use multiple voices – Switch between various "messengers" who may each address people in a different style that facilitates a high level of acceptance.
- Be clear – Set understandable expectations to avoid later misunderstanding and disappointment.
- Honesty is the only policy – Sooner or later people will find out the truth anyway, so do not hold it back.
- Use emotions, not just logic – you are dealing with human beings who have feelings about situations, which is something you can use to your advantage.
- Encourage – Change is always difficult; nevertheless, people have to feel good about the situation to be successful.
- Make the message tangible – Tell people specifically what will change for them and their work environment and what are the specific expectations?

- Listen, listen, listen – Your people likely know more about their processes and the consequences of change than you.

The basis to apply all these guidelines is the audience segmentation. Once you know exactly who you are addressing, you can optimize your information and communication activities accordingly, applying the presented guidelines. The following questions facilitate audience segmentation [6]:

- Who is in the segment?
- How will people be affected?
- What reaction will they have?
- What behavior will we need from them?
- How can we stimulate this behavior?
- When shall we inform/communicate?
- What medium should we use for each message?
- Who should communicate the message?

Challenges for successful change management activities result from the following aspects:

- Disbelief
- False familiarity
- Fear
- The "rumor mill"
- Incomprehensibility
- Abstraction
- Complexity
- Use of cliches

The business process factory of MPE can deliver the necessary content for the information and communication activities in form of business process models. The models can then be used as a common "language of change." The language of change facilitates the communication between various groups involved in a process change management initiative, such as business experts and managers, executives, IT experts, software vendors, and consultants. The use of formal methods, such as event-driven process chains (EPCs) helps to support clear, straightforward communication. These methods promote communication across company boundaries or between locations in various countries to avoid misunderstanding. The role of process models is explained in Fig. 4.6.

For example, a well-known beverage manufacturer uses process models widely as a communication basis. The company develops all job descriptions, based on process models. On the one hand, this ensures that the change documented in the models is actually implemented. On the other hand, it ensures that only realistic, achievable change suggestions are defined. Because the same business process models drive the people change management and the IT change, e.g. through an SOA environment, you end up in a holistic business process transformation.

To use those process models effectively for change management, the graphical representation of the models may have to be adjusted to the specific target segment

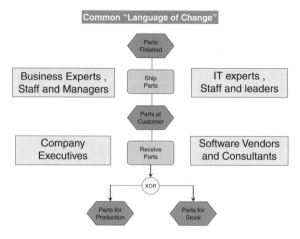

Fig. 4.6 Business process models as common language of change

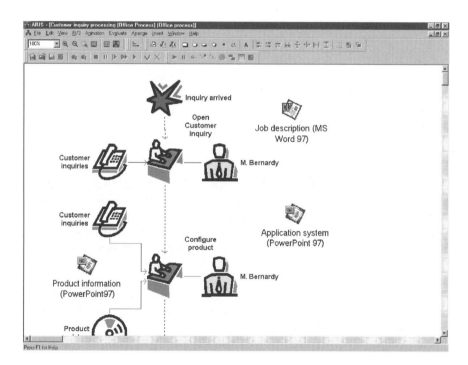

Fig. 4.7 Business process model in a less abstract format (in ARIS Design Platform)

of the information and communication activity. People who work in a warehouse or manufacturing environment may not be accustomed to process models consisting of rectangles, diamonds, ovals, and other abstract objects. They may even get anxious about them. Therefore, those abstract symbols could be replaced by more concrete objects, like a desk for a function or a picture of a person for an organizational unit. BPM tools used to support MPE deliver a transformation from one model representation to another automatically [10] without changing any semantic content. An example of such process models in a less abstract format using the design functionality of the ARIS Platform is shown in Fig. 4.7.

Because the business process models are in a digital format, they can be distributed via the Internet, again using the process factory modeling environment [10]. This enables fast distribution of information, as required by MPE, and the easy update of information because it is centralized in the process warehouse. This results in increased efficiency in the change management process.

In international company environments, cultural differences between locations in different countries must be taken into account. Therefore, different process model representation may be used in different countries. However, the semantic content of all those models remains the same, just the format changes.

The unique effects of the global business environment and their impacts on MPE will be discussed later.

Now, we will discuss the training activities in a business process change management initiative. Information and communication prepare the way for training regarding the new business processes.

4.3   How Do You Provide Process Training?

Training ensures that people can do their jobs as required by the altered or newly established business process. Training activities must also be organized with a business process-oriented approach and address the relevant changes of the existing as-is processes or the integration of a new process into the overall process landscape. Business process-oriented training can be divided into four major activities [11]:

- Basic training – business background
- Basic training – enabler (e.g., newly implemented application software)
- Business process training
- Kick-off training

In basic business training, the changing business background is explained. This allows people to understand the motivation for the change and ensures that they have the necessary general business knowledge. For example, a manufacturing company that previously executed material requirements planning (MRP) manually implements an ERP solution, including the use of MRP functionality. This means employees who formerly did straightforward calculations of required parts now have to decide how those parts should be ordered (e.g., based on a specific minimum stock or based on demand). They must set the appropriate parameters in the software application. The work requires more developed business skills, which are provided in the basic business training.

The basic "enabler" training is an introduction to new technologies or other enablers to be used in the changed processes. This training phase includes topics such as the handling of application software products or the use of new process performance tools. This training is less focused on "what to do" and more on "how to do things" in the future, in the changed business environment. In the past, this training phase was often considered very relevant. However, with easier to use IT systems, the importance of this training activity is less applicable.

The most important training phase is clearly business process training. This training empowers people to do their new or modified jobs in the changed process environment. These training activities explain how to apply the business knowledge using the new enablers in a business process to achieve the defined change. It basically involves all aspects concerning the execution of the new business processes, as well as monitoring and controlling this process. This training phase ensures that people have a minimum understanding of the end-to-end business process helping them to realize the impact of their work and the work of others involved in the process, and on the final result for an internal or external customer. This training phase makes the overall training approach a true business process training, a key element of MPE business process change management.

Kick-Off Training ensures that people recall the key aspects of the change, the dry-run for the process to "go-live." This training chiefly prepares people for the first time phase when the changed business environment may not be 100% stabilized, e.g., due to technical challenges. This includes information such as who to contact with questions or other work-arounds that may be necessary.

The structure of the business process-oriented training is shown in Fig. 4.8.

In many instances, the delivery of the necessary training is the greatest change management challenge for an enterprise. Frequently, thousands of people need training in new business processes and new enablers, such as ERP systems or new SOA-based processes. Therefore, the introduction of computer-based training (CBT) has become more and more important and often replaces face-to-face classroom training [12]. Although it is important to increase the efficiency of MPE, there may also be situations when face-to-face training is more appropriate. For example, it may be important to have spoken with some of the key experts personally to more easily ask questions at a later time. Also, face-to-face discussions are sometimes more

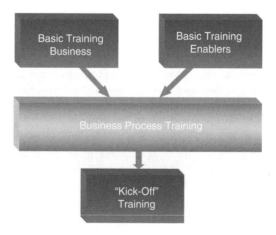

Fig. 4.8 Business process-oriented training

effective. Therefore, a hybrid training approach, combining CBT and face-to-face training, is an excellent solution.

In combination with CBT, concepts of distance learning using the Internet as enabler have also become increasingly more important [12–14]. This approach reduces logistical challenges tremendously and ensures constant and consistent training quality. Therefore, this approach is again very relevant to ensuring the efficiency of MPE. It has to be used in the right overall delivery mix for the various training sessions.

Distance learning via the Internet basically enables people to obtain the best education possible from wherever it is available. Universities in some countries may offer classes about the relevant business topics that are not available in other countries. This is no longer an issue. Enterprises have the choice [15]. They can use education offerings from institutions around the world via distance learning. MPE encourages the consideration and use of such options.

Much of the process training can also be integrated in the enabling technology itself, e.g. the SOA environment. People can view the process models and the process steps on which they are working as well as the next activities to be executed. They can get necessary background information, submit questions, and learn about the process. This results in individualized, on-the-job training focused on relevant business processes.

Such an approach of integrated training also supports the concept of lifetime learning. Continuous change in the business environment, leading to process change, requires continuous training. Training becomes part of day-to-day work. This is an important aspect for MPE because it ensures the continuous integration of strategy and execution, resulting in high performance.

For business process training, the use of virtual worlds could become an increasingly important method for delivery. As discussed, the process models of the MPE process factory could be used to configure a virtual environment where people can learn how to execute future processes. They "live" their future processes, just as pilots are trained using flight simulators [16].

4.4   The Bottom Line

- Business process change management is the combination of information, communication, and training regarding changes in existing business processes or the creation of new processes (Sect. 4.1).
- Change management ensures that the necessary actions are initiated with an acceptable delay, required actions are executed in a fast and effective way, and all reactions and actions are initiated and executed in a controlled manner to enable high performance (Sect. 4.1).
- The content of information, communication, and training concerning specific business processes can be structured using the ARIS Architecture (Sect. 4.1).

- Business process change management is a process in and of itself. Therefore, process-oriented methodologies and approaches can be applied. Business process management software can be used to support change management (Sect. 4.1).
- Information and communication in a business process change management approach should be well prepared, including specifically an audience segmentation (Sect. 4.2).
- The business process models delivered by MPE process design phase can be used as a common "language of change" (Sect. 4.2).
- To use those process models effectively for change management, it may be necessary to adjust the graphical representation of the models to the specific target segment (Sect. 4.2).
- Business process-oriented training can be divided into four major activities: basic training concerning the business background, basic training concerning used enablers, business process training, and kick-off training (Sect. 4.3).
- The most important training phase is the business process training. It explains how to apply the business knowledge using the new enablers in a business process to achieve the defined change (Sect. 4.3).
- A hybrid training approach, combining CBT and face-to-face training, is generally an excellent delivery mode. Also, concepts of distance learning using the Internet as enabler become increasingly important (Sect. 4.3).

References

1. Kirchmer, M, Scheer, A W: Change management – key for business process excellence. In: Scheer, A W, Abolhassan, E, Jost, W, Kirchmer, M (eds.) Business Process Change Management – ARIS in Practice, pp. 1–14. Springer, Berlin (2003)
2. Kalakota, R, Robinson, M: M-Business – The Race to Mobility. McGraw Hill, New York (2002)
3. Oleson, J: Pathways to Agility – Mass Customization in Action. Wiley, New York/Chichester (1998)
4. Spath, D., Baumeister, M., Barrho, T., Dill, C: Change management im Wandel. In: Industrie Management – Zeitschrift fuer industrielle Geschaeftsprozesse, pp. 9–13 (2001)
5. Collins, J: Good to Great – Why Some Companies Make the Leap.. .and Others Don't. HarperCollins, New York (2001)
6. Hammer, M, Stanton, S: The Reengineering Revolution. HarperCollins, Glasgow (1995)
7. Scheer, A W: ARIS – Business Process Frameworks, 2nd edn. Springer, Berlin (1998)
8. Scheer, A W: ARIS – Business Process Modeling, 2nd edn. Springer, Berlin (1998)
9. Exel, S, Wilms, S: Change management with ARIS. In: Scheer, A W, Abolhassan, E, Jost, W, Kirchmer, M (eds.) Business Process Change Management – ARIS in Practice, pp. 23–18. Springer, Berlin (2003)
10. IDS Scheer, A.G. (ed.): ARIS Platform. Product Brochure. Saarbruecken, (2007)
11. Kirchmer, M: Business Process Oriented Implementation of Standard Software – How to Achieve Competitive Advantage Efficiently and Effectively, 2nd edn. Springer, Berlin (1999)
12. Kraemer, W., Mueller, M.: Virtuelle corporate university – executive education architecture and knowledge management. In: Scheer, A.W. (Ed.): Electronic Business und Knowledge

Management – Neue Dimensionen fuer den Unternehmenserfolg, pp. 491–525. Heidelberg (1999)

13. Kirchmer, M.: e-Business Process Improvement (eBPI): Building and managing collaborative e-business scenarios. In: Callaos, N., Loutfi, M., Justan, M.: Proceedings of the 6th World Multiconference on Systemics, Cybernetics and Informatics, vol. 8, pp. 387–396. Orlando (2002)

14. Kraemer, W., Gallenstein, C, Sprendger, P.: Learning management fuer Fuehrungskraefte. In: Industrie Management – Zeitschrift fuer industrielle Geschaeftsprozesse, pp. 55–59 (2001)

15. Fingar, P: Extreme Competition – Innovation and the Great 21st Century Business Reformation. Meghan-Kiffer, Tampa (2006)

16. Greenbaum, J.: SimEnterprise: the video gamer's guide to SAP's business-process revolution. In: SAP NetWeaver Magazine, vol. 2 (2006)

Chapter 5
Business Process Governance for MPE

Today, many enterprises still use concepts of business process management (BPM) for one-time improvement projects and short-term initiatives. An increasing number of organizations, however, recognize its power as a fundamental management discipline, which can be instrumental in achieving strategic goals for competitive advantage and long-term survival. This demands discipline that must be ensured on a permanent basis. The process of management of process excellence (MPE) has to be managed from day to day. For BPM to work effectively, organizations must orchestrate its "management," also known as business process governance (BPG). This ensures the proper design, implementation, execution, and controlling of processes through MPE; therefore, it enables the process life cycle management of MPE and the achievement of high performance.

Andrew Spanyi, a well-known expert in BPM and the author of several books, and I have worked closely together on the topic of BPG. I had approached the field of BPG from a general trend and required infrastructure point of view, while he had focused on necessary leadership behavior. We discussed the topic and decided to combine the various aspects: leadership, technology, and methodology aspects [1, 2]. The findings of our research are basis for the discussions in this chapter.

BPG represents the overarching guidelines for the administration and application of BPM. It defines the allocation of power and authority in the enterprise. Business trends, corporate strategies, legal requirements, and other aspects, like the use of specific standard software packages, influence the design of process governance. BPG sets the stage for the establishment and use of next-generation process-automation environments, such as SOA, at the enterprise level. It is also essential for effective change management. The development of appropriate leadership behavior is important for sustainable success.

BPG is a key element of an organization's process strategy. This positioning is shown in Fig. 5.1.

You may wonder why this important strategic concept was not introduced earlier in this book. The reason is because it is easier to comprehend the concept and impact of BPG with an understanding of the approach of MPE and the impact of its innovation goal, as well as IT and people topics. There are many aspects to consider

M. Kirchmer, *High Performance Through Process Excellence*,
DOI 10.1007/978-3-642-21165-2_5, © Springer-Verlag Berlin Heidelberg 2011

Fig. 5.1 Focus on process strategy of MPE

when you manage a successful BPM approach in an organization, which is why a specific governance approach is necessary.

But what exactly is BPG and why do you really need it? We will now discuss the answers to these questions.

5.1 Business Process Governance: What Is It and Why Do You Need it?

BPG is a set of guidelines focused on organizing all BPM activities and initiatives of an organization to manage all of its business processes. The resulting governance framework provides the frame of reference to guide organizational units of an enterprise and ensures responsibility and accountability for adhering to the BPM approach. In its simplest terms, BPG can be considered the "definition" layer of BPM and contributes to the definition and allocation of power and authority in the enterprise by specifying the governance framework. BPG involves the following components:

- A high-level model of an organization's key processes
- Clarification of high-level goals to frame the definition of KPIs that will be used to monitor the performance of these business processes
- Accountability for the improvement and management of business processes
- A clear formal structure for the description of business processes and the related aspects (enterprise or business process architecture)
- An outline of the infrastructure necessary for BPM
- Aligned recognition and reward systems
- The set of priorities in improving key business processes

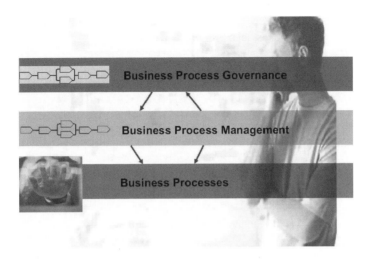

Fig. 5.2 Business process governance: Managing business process management

The primary objective of BPG is to set the stage for the effective deployment of BPM to create value for customers, shareholders, and other stakeholders. BPG ensures that BPM delivers consistent business results to satisfy and exceed the expectations of an organization. Thus, BPG "governs" BPM. It is responsible for the management of the BPM process. BPM again drives the success of all other business processes, specifically core processes relevant for a company's competitive positioning. The interactions between BPG, BPM, and an organization's remaining business processes are visualized in Fig. 5.2. The relation between BPG and BPM is explained in detail in Fig. 5.3.

Some BPG guidelines can again be processes. Let us look at a simple example regarding a restaurant that we want to manage in a process-oriented way. Two governance processes are depicted. The first process requests the automation of a business process, but also requires the definition of a manual backup process to reduce or eliminate the risk inherent to process automation. The second governance process presents the scenario for the manual process to be used, and should the automation technology malfunction and the backup process needs to be executed to ensure the delivery of the process result. These governance processes encourage efficient, automated processes, and simultaneously mitigate the risk of process automation. The governance processes, in the format of event-driven process chains (EPC [3]), are shown in Fig. 5.4. The diamonds represent business events, the green rectangles functions, the ovals organizational units, and the yellow rectangles are information objects.

In the process design of BPM, those BPG processes lead to the design of process models for efficient automation. The backup processes are manual, independent of the implemented technologies. Examples are shown in Fig. 5.5.

In this example, a waiter takes the orders from patrons and transfers them through a PDA directly to the bar and the kitchen, so they can prepare the beverages

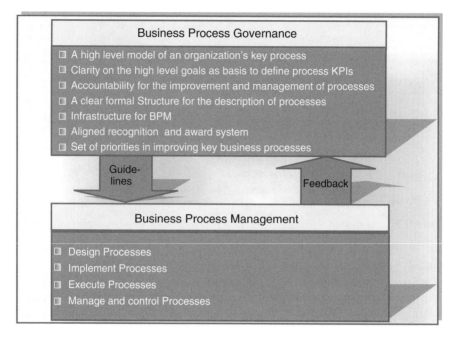

Fig. 5.3 Relation of BPG and business process management

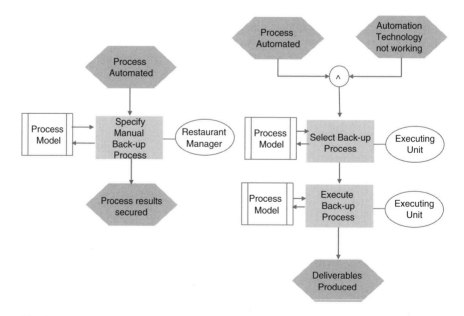

Fig. 5.4 Examples of governance processes for a restaurant

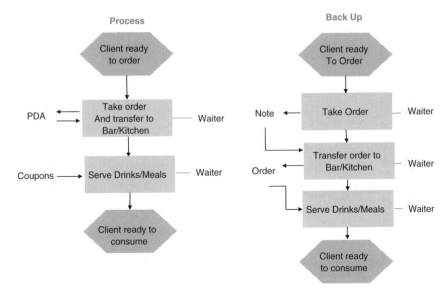

Fig. 5.5 Example of restaurant processes from the business process management design phase

and meals for the customer. If the PDA malfunctions, the waiter executes the process manually with pen and paper. In both scenarios, the customer receives the ordered products. However, the manual processes are more time consuming, inefficient, and susceptible to human error, and hamper productivity.

In reality, if a patron visits our restaurant, the business processes are executed, based on the designed processes. The models developed in our BPM approach are carried out. If possible, the waiter ensures the efficient process using the PDA. In the case of a technical problem, he also knows how to proceed to fulfill the customer demands.

BPG is relevant for all phases of BPM and specifically in all phases of MPE design, implementation, execution, as well as monitoring and controlling of processes. Each phase of BPM is guided by BPG, leading to its overall orchestration. These guidelines may target the content of process models (e.g., identifying and mitigating risks) or purely formal aspects of BPM (e.g., each function of a process model must be assigned to the responsible and accountable organizational unit). This is visualized in Fig. 5.6.

An example of a BPG guideline for process design is "graphically identify operational risk in process models." A process implementation example is "deploying the related business application software (ERP, SCM, CRM, etc.) to support the business processes" [4] (resulting in a "process-oriented implementation"). "Any change of the process workflow must be approved by the managers of the involved departments" is an example of a guideline for process execution. "Benchmarks for process KPIs have to be checked and, if necessary, updated every 6 months" guides the continuous process improvement in the controlling phase of MPE.

What is the broader background of BPG? BPG is the required foundation to assure the sustainability of process improvements and the continuous focus on creating value for all stakeholders, such as customers, business partners, employees, and

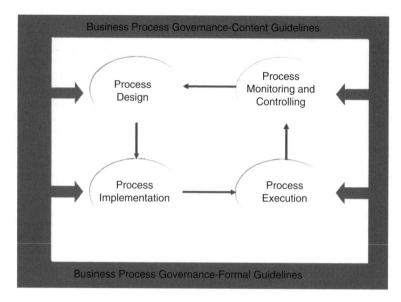

Fig. 5.6 Process governance: guidelines for each phase of business process management

shareholders. The importance of governance has already been recognized in one-time improvements to individual business processes, such as order to cash, source to pay, or new product development. Its importance increases significantly when an organization decides to deploy BPM on an enterprise level for competitive advantage.

BPG ensures and guides the enterprise-specific execution of BPM. It is an essential component of leadership; therefore, general principles for execution of strategies and management tasks must be considered when defining BPG for an organization [5]:

- Know your people and your business
- Insist on realism
- Set clear goals and priorities
- Follow through
- Reward the doers
- Expand the capabilities of your employees

To develop BPG for an organization, it is crucial that the leadership team knows the people and the business of an enterprise within the context of key business processes. A focus on realism and achieving a shared understanding of the organization's business processes is required when developing BPG guidelines; otherwise, the guidelines are worthless. At a minimum, the leadership team must have a common understanding of the high-level business processes, including clarity on organizational responsibilities, deliverables, inputs, outputs, key functional steps, dependencies, and KPIs. Within BPG, clear goals and priorities must be set so that people's efforts in executing BPM activities are as effective as possible – and provide best value. These priorities are often defined in a BPM roadmap, identifying the "target processes" for improvement and the necessary BPM capabilities to achieve them [6]. BPG ensures that business performance management activities create value and the "doers" or people who get them done are rewarded. This really makes BPM a part of how the organization completes work. BPG should include guidelines for training and education to expand the capabilities of employees, and call attention to the importance of cross-functional collaboration to properly equip people involved in BPM.

The leaders of organizations that chose to deploy BPM as a management discipline appreciate that value is created and work is accomplished via the organization's business processes. They recognize the importance of BPM to topics, such as strategy, growth, and the integration of mergers and acquisitions. These topics typically preoccupy the thoughts of leadership teams – the people of an organization responsible for making MPE happen – in high-performance businesses.

Thoughtful leaders recognize that BPM enables the clearer formulation and execution of strategy. As far back as 1985, Michael Porter emphasized the concept of the value chain and noted, "Activities, then, are the basics of competitive advantage. Overall advantage or disadvantage results from all of a company's activities, not only a few" and then went on to say, "The essence of strategy is choosing to perform activities differently than rivals do" [7]. Strategy must be based on a thorough assessment of the external and internal environments. Organizational strategy drives the design of BPG and BPM enables the execution of strategy. This aspect supports MPE's key role as the link between strategy and operations, which will drive high performance for the organization.

When it comes to sustainable organic growth and innovation, leaders also recognize that BPM is equally important. Rapid, sustainable growth requires a systemic view of the business and broad collaboration, which requires immense effort from many firms. The design of BPG must recognize that focusing on goals, such as flawless delivery responsiveness, is essential in providing existing products or services to existing or new markets.

When growth is planned through mergers or acquisitions, the integration phase is essential to success. Perceptive leaders appreciate that an important reason for the success of mergers or acquisitions is the ability of the merged firm to perform for and meet the needs of their customers. It is in the "integration phase" that BPM can play an enabling role. This is related to the fact that merged firms often have an opportunity to gather specific information on comparative core business processes and their relative health and address customer-facing issues in the premerger due diligence period.

BPG plays a key role in MPE and enabling high performance for an enterprise. Organizations elect to invest energy in establishing BPG because it is the management infrastructure that enables them to address critical topics, such as strategy, growth, and the integration of mergers and acquisitions through the improvement and management of the corporation's core business processes. BPG sets the stage to achieve competitive advantage through BPM.

In the previously described concept of the Enterprise 2.0+, BPG must be adapted by focusing on goals and general directions regarding the MPE activities, while still addressing the aforementioned topics. BPG has to offer sufficient freedom – and also sufficient direction – to people to truly use the benefits of Web 2.0 capabilities. Creativity and collaboration need to be applied to achieve the organization's goals and provide value to the relevant stakeholders.

So, how does an organization establish BPG? What is necessary to ensure BPG?

5.2 How Do You Establish Business Process Governance?

BPG is the cornerstone for establishing BPM in an organization. There are three essential activities to begin BPG, a subset of the previously discussed components of BPG:

- High-level enterprise process model that identifies the key process of an organization
- Set of goals to frame the definition of KPIs
- Management plan, including an enterprise or process architecture structure, priorities, as well as the organizational structure for people involved in BPM activities

The other components of BPG must be added over time, depending on the specific needs of an organization. In general, enterprises require a set of leadership behaviors that facilitate the development of critical BPG components and contribute directly to the effectiveness of BPM.

The development of a robust, compelling, and visually striking enterprise-level business process model is one of the key components of BPG. In the absence of such a model, leadership teams will rely on the one model that most companies do have – the organizational chart – and that will unduly and adversely influence their thinking. In most cases, this will result in a traditional, functional approach with all of its disadvantages. The enterprise-level definition of processes includes core, support, and management processes [8], as well as the necessary governance processes.

Primary processes are typically customer touching (e.g., "order-to-cash" and "new product development"). Supporting processes typically enable the performance of the primary customer-touching processes. Examples of supporting processes include "hire-to-retire," "financial reporting," and "information technology development." Management processes generally create the framework for BPM (e.g., "budget development" and "performance monitoring"). BPG delivers the governance processes relevant to manage BPM activities. We discussed such examples previously.

The development of KPIs for the set of business processes in the enterprise-level process model must involve balance between what is important to customers (and their enterprises) and what is important to the company itself. This is dramatically different than what occurs in conventional organizations, where traditional financial measures of revenue, expenses, earnings, and cash flow dominate. The metrics that really matter to customers, such as "on-time receipt of product or service," "complete, defect-free delivery," "an accurate and user-friendly invoice," "rapid and courteous responsiveness," or similar KPIs often are not included in the front page of the executive dashboard or scorecard. In traditional companies, even when the metrics that matter to customers are monitored, the next level of diagnostic measurement is usually missing and the infrastructure for corrective action is either lacking or flawed.

In contrast, the development of BPG requires a broad range of KPIs, including cost, quality, timeliness, and productivity metrics, in the measurement of the key deliverables for each enterprise-level process, and the means to cascade these performance metrics to the subprocess level. Furthermore, a realistic assessment of current performance is needed for each end-to-end process.

The combination of the clear definition of enterprise-level processes in the process model and the clarity on KPIs are prerequisites for the management plan, which is the third basic component in establishing BPG. The process management plan must answer three fundamental questions:

- Which of our business processes need to be improved, by how much and by when, in order for us to achieve our goals?
- Who will be accountable for the improvement and management of each key business process?
- How will we organize to fully engage our people in the improvement and management of key business processes?

To determine which business processes need to be improved, by how much and by when, in order to achieve which business goals, the leadership team needs to express its business goals in a process context and assess the size of the gap between current performance and desired performance [6]. This involves making difficult choices to prioritize key projects and resource allocation. Similarly, key decisions need to be made to determine the executive accountability for the improvement and management of business processes and the development of the appropriate process management structure. Although there are various approaches to assigning accountability or ownership, the two most common might be called the "two hats line" and the "one hat staff approach. In the "two hats line" approach, a senior line executive assumes responsibility for an end-to-end process, as well as retaining accountability for his or her functional area. Clearly, this approach relies on "matrix management" principles. In the "one hat staff" approach, a senior executive is appointed to a staff position of "process owner" or "process steward" for an end-to-end business process.

A centralized organizational unit ensuring the implementation and execution of BPG is generally necessary. This group of people also has to support the employees involved in daily BPM-related management and administration activities. For example, a "Center of Excellence" managed by a chief process officer (CPO), could be founded. It is essential to have an organizational unit responsible for the management of BPM and execution of BPG itself. We will discuss the set up of such a center of Excellence later in this chapter.

To apply the defined enterprise process model on a company-wide level, this model should be the entrance point into a structured design of processes on all levels of detail. This can be supported by enterprise architecture (EA), which is a framework to describe all aspects relevant for a business process on various levels of detail. Examples for predefined architectures are the ARIS Architecture, the Zachman Framework or the US Department of Defense Architecture Framework (DoDAF) [3, 9–12].

In most cases, those general frameworks are then adjusted to company-specific needs. The following key activities are used to build an EA in an organization:

- Define architecture requirements (e.g., which aspects of a process should be included: business, IT, legal, etc.)
- Select the right existing EA framework (ARIS, DoDAF, Zachman, etc.)
- Tailor the selected architecture (which information is needed in which level of detail)
- Choose the right methods/notations (methods that deliver the needed information, easy to use, etc.)
- Select the appropriate architecture software tool to implement the framework

The application of an EA is facilitated through software systems, such as the ARIS Platform [13, 14], a BPM software environment that can be used to support MPE. EA can be seen as a tool to transmit BPG into the operational BPM. This is visualized in Fig. 5.7.

The definition of BPG is generally influenced by the following factors:

- Enterprise strategy (e.g., customer-centric organization, real-time business, cost reduction, highest quality standards, or specific innovation goals)

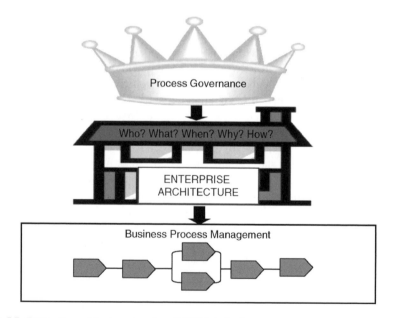

Fig. 5.7 Enterprise architecture: transfer of BPG into business process management

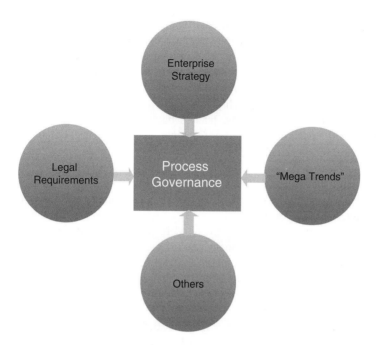

Fig. 5.8 Influence factors on process governance

- Legal requirements (e.g., Sarbanes-Oxley (SOX), Basel II, or FDA regulations)
- "Megatrends" (e.g., globalization, mobility, or enterprise networks)
- Other corporate factors (e.g., ERP systems in use, enterprise culture, or regional locations)

These factors are shown in Fig. 5.8. Once the general influence factors for BPG are identified, concrete requirements must be defined. Some requirements are relevant for all enterprises within an industry sector or even across industry boundaries – others are company specific. Therefore, it is very important for each enterprise to develop a specific BPG, suited to the specific culture and business situation.

The development of BPG to govern an organization's BPM efforts is still not a general management practice, although more and more organizations are moving in this direction. In many cases, companies start establishing BPG without calling it by name. For example, they develop method handbooks as part of their BPM projects. However, a systematic BPM approach also requires the clear development of BPG.

In spite of the compelling logic that customer and shareholder value is created by means of business processes, current leaders at many companies continue to support a traditional, functional view of the business. Why? There are at least four possible reasons [15, 16]: Leaders do not care; Leaders cannot focus; Leaders do not know how; Leaders have been conditioned.

If leaders really cared, focused, and knew how, would not they behave differently? Would not they measure what is important to customers in a disciplined way, in addition to monitoring the traditional financial metrics, such as revenues, earnings, and cash flow? Would not they assign accountability for the performance of the company's large business processes, instead of opting to assign accountability purely in terms of functional or business unit lines? Of course leaders would do these things if they cared enough to invest the time and energy, were able to devote sufficient attention for sustainability, and knew how to do so.

However, in many companies, leaders have been conditioned by both their academic and business experience to think and act in traditional, functional terms. Most leaders studied a particular academic discipline in college, such as marketing, finance, IT, or engineering. Then, for most, their first job was in the same functional area that they studied – marketing, finance, IT, or engineering. In most cases, career progression was based on demonstrating excellence in that same area of functional responsibility.

It is this experience that leads to "silo" behavior and "turf protection." So it should come as no surprise that many leaders view the world through a functional bias. Although more and more universities and academic institutions are offering BPM-related educational programs, this is still not the norm. But things are starting to change, and process orientation is increasingly recognized as key for graduate and postgraduate education.

Leaders who chose to deploy BPG and BPM recognize the importance of shifting traditional functional thinking at both executive and middle-management levels. They practice a set of leadership behaviors to shift conventional wisdom and invest significant time and energy in this respect. This is the leadership aspect of BPG.

Leading firms appear to practice the following three distinct leadership behaviors in establishing BPG:

- Wide-ranging communication of a robust, enterprise-level process definition
- Discipline in performance measurement
- Commitment to broad-based education on BPM

The first leadership behavior in establishing BPG involves leadership commitment to a wide-ranging communication of a robust, enterprise-level process definition, and EA. A prerequisite is a compelling, visually striking enterprise process model and clarity on the ownership of the principal business processes depicted in this model. Such a process model is central to broad-based communication, but it is the leadership team's shared understanding of the underlying details on the definition of the business processes and the size of the performance gap that needs to be bridged that drives deep commitment to deploying BPM as a management practice.

The second essential leadership behavior in establishing and sustaining BPG is to exercise discipline in performance measurement and achieve balance between measuring what matters to customers and what matters to the company. Then the leadership team exercises discipline in reviewing results on a regular basis and takes corrective action when actual results are below targeted levels.

The next key leadership behavior in establishing and sustaining BPG is related to leadership commitment to broad-based education on BPM. In leading firms, executives are directly involved in sponsoring, introducing, and even delivering process-oriented education to senior and middle managers.

Although the set of these three leadership behaviors requires a significant investment of executive time and energy, the return on effort invested can be considerable. What does it mean to maintain BPG and, with that, ensure long-term, successful BPM in an organization?

5.3 What Does It Mean to Maintain Process Governance?

The central goal of BPG is to ensure that BPM delivers consistent business results to satisfy and exceed the expectations of customers and shareholders for high performance. Thus, BPG "governs" BPM on a day-to-day basis. The resulting management and administrative activities must be part of the daily business.

Success in establishing and sustaining BPG, and hence BPM, relies on both leadership attitudes, as discussed above, and organizational skill in the deployment of the required management discipline. In terms of maintaining BPG, IT matters tremendously. Not only is it important to use a process-modeling system as previously discussed, it is equally important that the selected software is able to link directly to a company's execution environment, which can be ERP or SOA based or follow the Enterprise 2.0+ as an IT architectural framework. The degree of complexity in most businesses requires the use of a robust modeling tool to effectively define and cascade BPG principles through the BPM activities.

BPG enables the discussed concept of open BPM [17] within MPE by requesting and identifying open standards to be used. These selections must be reviewed on a regular basis to reflect the newest developments regarding technology and business standards. The measurement of defined KPIs can also be automated [13]. This ensures the effective implementation of BPG guidelines in a cost- and time-efficient way [13].

The definition of BPG processes and guidelines for each phase of the BPM approach can be used to drive an "execution-oriented" culture of an enterprise [5]. BPG sets the stage for getting things done. An enterprise must define how BPG affects the organizational structure. BPG-related activities may be centralized for the entire organization or decentralized (e.g., in business units). Alternatively, a combination of both extreme approaches can be applied. The decision about the centralization or decentralization of BPG activities can be made on the basis of the same principles used in BPM [4]:

- Coordination requirements
- Relevant time periods
- Actuality of data (yearly, monthly, etc.)
- Data volume

The organization of BPG may lead to new departments like "BPM Centers of Excellence" or to new positions, e.g., the formerly mentioned CPO, Process

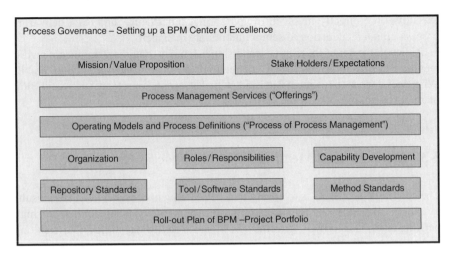

Fig. 5.9 Steps necessary to set up a BPM Center of Excellence

owners, Process Architects, Process Analysts, Process Repository Administrator, and more. The steps necessary to set up such a Center of Excellence are shown in Fig. 5.9.

It is important to define such a Center of Excellence in a "market-driven way", considering the company as its "internal market." By defining internal offerings that such a center brings to the organization, it stays relevant and is not just seen as an overhead. The head of this center is basically the owner of the process of process management. The center itself provides the BPM governance and executes key components of the process of process management.

The implementation and execution of BPG is also enabled by specific governance applications (e.g., Sarbanes-Oxley (SOX) Audit Management Systems), similar to how BPM is supported by BPM applications and the execution of processes by systems like ERP. Some of the software applications also serve as governance applications. This application hierarchy is visualized in Fig. 5.10.

BPG applications require appropriate implementation approaches. Although the general concepts of a process-oriented implementation of standard software can be utilized [4], the following specific aspects must be included in the BPG application approach:

- Close integration with BPM tools (e.g., a BPG application could be a module of a BPM tool carrying out a consistency check of process models.)
- Documentation requirements to proof the compliance with BPG processes and guidelines (e.g., executing SOX-relevant checks is insufficient – these requirements must also be documented.)
- Change management to make BPG part of the overall enterprise culture (e.g., BPG guidelines may also need to be applied "manually" by employees working on BPM initiatives; thus, BPG tools simply deliver the necessary information.)
- Other aspects (e.g., the requirement to use formal methods and tools)

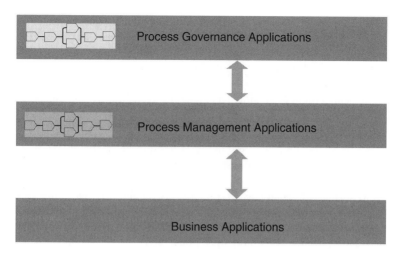

Fig. 5.10 Software application hierarchy, starting with process governance software

BPG is a key element of operational and tactical enterprise management. It ensures the appropriate and targeted use of BPM throughout the entire business process life cycle. Therefore, it has to be maintained on a day-to-day basis as part of an organization's daily working activities.

5.4 The Bottom Line

- BPG is a set of guidelines focused on organizing all BPM activities and initiatives of an organization to manage its business processes (Sect. 5.1).
- BPG ensures that BPM delivers consistent business results to satisfy and exceed the expectations of an organization for high performance (Sect. 5.1).
- Some of the guidelines of BPG can again be processes, so-called BPG processes. They can be managed using a BPM approach (Sect. 5.1).
- The leaders of organizations that chose to deploy BPM as a management discipline appreciate its value, and therefore, establish BPG. They recognize its importance to topics such as strategy, growth, and the integration of mergers and acquisitions (Sect. 5.1).
- There are three essential components involved in getting BPG started: high-level enterprise process model, set of goals and a management plan, including an EA structure and the organizational structure for people involved in BPM activities (Sect. 5.2).
- Enterprises require a set of leadership behaviors that facilitate the development of critical BPG components and contribute directly to the effectiveness of BPM (Sect. 5.2).

- To apply the enterprise process model on a company-wide basis, this model should be the entry point into a structured design of processes on all levels of detail. This can be supported by an enterprise architecture (EA) (Sect. 5.2).
- The definition of BPG is influenced by multiple factors, including the enterprise strategy, legal requirements, and "megatrends" (Sect. 5.2).
- Leaders who chose to deploy BPG and BPM recognize the importance of shifting traditional functional thinking at both executive and middle management levels (Sect. 5.2).
- Success in establishing and sustaining BPG, and hence BPM, relies both on leadership attitudes and organizational skill in the deployment of the required management discipline (Sect. 5.3).
- A BPM Center of Excellence is required to provide the necessary BPG and execute the process of process management (Sect. 5.3).
- In terms of executing and maintaining BPG, IT matters tremendously and can be used to enforce some BPG guidelines (Sect. 5.3).
- BPG applications (specific software to support BPG) require appropriate implementation approaches (Sect. 5.3).

References

1. Kirchmer, M: Business Process Governance: Orchestrating the Management of BPM. White paper, Berwyn (2005)
2. Kirchmer, M., Spanyi, A.: Business Process Governance. White paper, 2nd revised edition. Berwyn (2007)
3. Scheer, A-W: ARIS – Business Process Modeling, 2nd edn. Springer, Berlin/New York/ Others (1998)
4. Kirchmer, M: Business Process Oriented Implementation of Standard Software – How to Achieve Competitive Advantage Efficiently and Effectively, 2nd edn. Springer, Berlin/ New York/Others (1999)
5. Bossidy, L, Charan, R: Execution: The Discipline of Getting Things Done. Basic Books, New York (2002)
6. Franz, P.: Developing a Process Agenda for Value-driven BPM. Point of View document. Accenture, London (2011)
7. Porter, M.: What is strategy? Harvard Business Review, November–December 1996
8. Rummler, G, Brache, Al: Improving Performance: Managing the White Space on the Organization Chart. Jossey-Bass, San Francisco (1990)
9. Scheer, A-W: ARIS – Business Process Frameworks, 2nd edn. Springer, Berlin/New York/ Others (1998)
10. O'Rourke, C, Fishman, N, Selkow, W: Enterprise Architecture Using the Zachman Framework. Thomson Course Technology, Boston (2003)
11. Lapkin, A.: The seven fatal mistakes of enterprise architecture. In: Gartner Research publication, ID-Number: GOO 126144, 22 Feb 2005
12. McGovern, J, Ambler, S W, Stevens, M E, Linn, J, Sharan, V, Jo, E K: A Practical Guide to Enterprise Architecture. Prentice Hall, Upper Saddle River (2004)
13. IDS Scheer AG (ed.): ARIS platform. Product Brochure. Saarbruecken (2007)
14. IDS Scheer, A G (ed.): ARIS Design Platform – ARIS Enterprise Architecture Solution. White paper, Saarbruecken (2006)

15. Spanyi, A: Business Process Management Is a Team Sport – Play It to Win. Anclote Press, Tampa (2003)
16. Spanyi, A: More for Less – The Power of Process Management. Meghan-Kiffer, Tampa (2006)
17. Kirchmer, M.: Knowledge communication empowers SOA for business agility. In: The 11th World Multi-Conference on Systemics, Cybernetics and Informatics, Proceedings, volume. III, pp. 301–307. Orlando, July 8–11, 2007

Chapter 6
Reference Models to Empower MPE

Process design is a key phase of management of process excellence (MPE). The resulting blueprint is the basis for the implementation and the execution, as well as the monitoring and controlling of processes. The use of flexible execution environments, such as SOA, particularly requires business process models in high-quality syntactical and semantic formats. Ensuring such modeling quality can be very time consuming. The use of appropriate process-modeling tools and process templates that are adapted to company-specific requirements can help tremendously. The use of process templates increases the efficiency and effectiveness of that process design phase significantly. The process templates are generally called "business process reference models."

Reference models facilitate the achievement of high-quality design while keeping the necessary resources at an acceptable level. Therefore, the use of reference models is an important element of MPE. They are key enablers of the process design phase.

While working in Japan for IDS Scheer, I started an initiative to develop a reference model for the pharmaceutical industry on the basis of specific documentation and reporting requirements, a model that would also reflect the related capabilities of SAP's enterprise resource planning (ERP) System. We were able to sell the product to clients and could use it ourselves successfully in consulting engagements, which proved that such "content products" were becoming increasingly important in supporting BPM initiatives. Accenture has built a major BPM Reference Model repository with over 20,000 models describing 71 industries. This enables a continuously increased value for Accenture's clients as those clients strive to achieve high performance. Process reference models truly increase efficiency and lead to higher-quality results.

This chapter will define reference models and focus specifically on business process reference models. It discusses how to procure reference models and learn how to use them in practice. The focus of this chapter, the process design of MPE, is shown in Fig. 6.1.

Process reference models show how process knowledge can be formalized and structured as a step toward knowledge transfer into a "product" that can be sold on

M. Kirchmer, *High Performance Through Process Excellence*,
DOI 10.1007/978-3-642-21165-2_6, © Springer-Verlag Berlin Heidelberg 2011

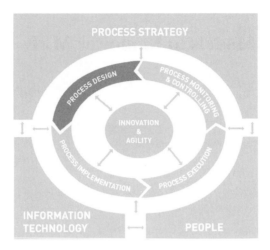

Fig. 6.1 Focus on process design of MPE

the market. Just as enterprises today purchase application software, in the future they may procure content in form of reference models.

6.1   What Are Reference Models and Why Should You Use Them?

Let us assume that you would like to design your procurement process, using the process factory in the MPE design phase. This process is not of particular importance and you do not expect to achieve any competitive advantage through its design. Therefore, it is sufficient to follow industry best practice. But how do you know what that industry best practice is? How can you complete necessary process models quickly and cost efficiently? This is where reference models can help.

Reference models (RMs) are generic conceptual models that formalize recommended practices for a special domain [1–3]. Therefore, they have the following characteristics [1–5]:

- Representation of best practices: RMs provide best practices for doing business.
- Universal applicability: RMs deliver business content well beyond an individual issue. Hence, they will not only be used for one enterprise, but a whole set of enterprises.
- Reusability: RMs are conceptual frameworks that can be easily reused in many information system projects. They are structured for easy adaptability to company-specific situations.

This means that RMs deliver best-practice information that can be used many times (e.g., in multiple organizations or for different projects). Their format allows easy application to specific situations. Therefore, they are, in general, available in digital form, e.g., files of process modeling software systems. Although the currently available RMs often do not completely fulfill all of those characteristics [4], they at least come close to those requirements.

In the context of MPE, we will apply "business process RMs." The RMs consist of "conceptual models" that are relevant for business processes, primarily even process models (complemented by models for other views on processes-like functions, data, or organization). In this chapter, we use RM as synonym for business process RMs.

In the procurement business process example explained earlier, one could use an industry best-practice RMs that includes a suggestion for the procurement. This enables the use of industry knowledge in an efficient and effective way, reduces the design time, and assures the desired design quality.

RMs represent content of various domains. According to those domains, one can distinguish different types of RM. The most important are the following:

- Industry RM: They represent best practices of a specific industry sector (e.g., a banking RM or a consumer packaged goods RM).
- Software RM: They describe best practice processes on the basis of a specific application software system. These could be traditional applications, such as ERP systems, or RM representing the subprocess supported by a service of an SOA.
- Procedural RM: They show best practices of specific procedures that are not part of the daily operational business of an organization (e.g., a project management RM or an RM to build business process governance).
- Company RM: These models represent a best practice within a company or a company group (e.g., a sales process that is rolled out to all sales subsidiaries of the organization).

In many cases, RMs represent a combination of two or more model types. For example, RM could be an ERP-based reference model (e.g., for SAP software) for the consumer packaged goods industry, including special aspects, like a "direct store delivery" process. The different types of RMs are visualized in Fig. 6.2.

The use of RMs provides business benefits in the process design, such as:

- Cost reduction
- Time reduction
- Quality improvement
- Risk reduction
- Transparency
- Common language
- Basis for benchmarking

Since "premanufactured" models can be used, the development cost for company-specific process models is reduced. This also reduces development time. It is much faster to discuss how to modify a process model to adapt it to a company-specific situation than to develop it from scratch. The anticipated high-quality modeling

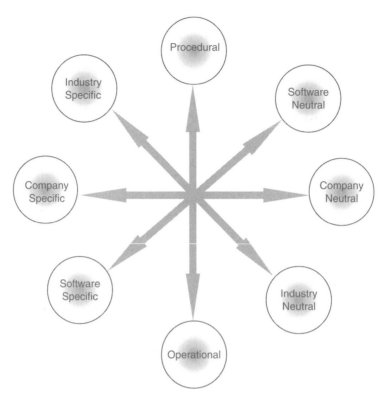

Fig. 6.2 Types of business process reference models

of RM leverages this quality standard for enterprise-specific process-modeling activities. This is true for syntactical as well as for semantic aspects. The content of RM is already validated; hence, its application leads to risk reduction. A knowledge domain described by RM becomes transparent through the clear and easy-to-read structure of RM. RM defines also the terms used in the model, hence they can be the basis for a common language, e.g., in inter-enterprise projects with team members of different companies. If several enterprises use the same RM as a basis to structure their business processes, this facilitates the benchmarking of those processes later.

Summarizing those effects, RMs lead to efficient process design, effective execution, and therefore, the increased agility of an organization. This is visualized in Fig. 6.3.

This is exactly the effect required by MPE RM enable smart decisions and fast execution. They effectively link strategy to execution in an organization, being focused on the key phase of MPE – process design.

So, where can one find such RMs? Are there specialized vendors like can be found for packaged software?

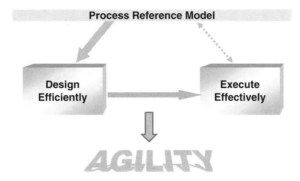

Fig. 6.3 Agility through business process reference models

6.2   How to Obtain RMs?

RMs are basically products that you use to build business processes, just as you use other products such as software or hardware. In a broad sense, all of those products can be procured through the IT market.

Let us review briefly the development of this market of information systems and technology. In the 1970s, the dominating products were hardware – computers. Once the hardware was selected, the software was developed or procured accordingly. This changed in the 1990s with the appearance of ERP systems. Suddenly, the main attention shifted to software products, especially to standard application software. Hardware became more or less a commodity. Because the business content of some of those standard software systems was already documented in form of RM [6], the market for business content in form of RM started to develop. I expect that this market will increase significantly in the next few years. Because SOA offers organizations increased flexibility, the necessary business content, to manage and use this flexibility efficiently, has to be procured separately. Otherwise, the development of major process-oriented software systems may become too cost and time intensive. This development is shown in Fig. 6.4.

Many of the RMs available today are not sold as standalone products. They are either provided together with other products (e.g., software systems or consulting offerings) or as part of a membership service (e.g., of a non-for-profit organization). However, I expect that the "productization" of RM will progress rapidly. Consulting and software companies could have major business units delivering RM-based products. Accenture has already gone this direction and is in the mean time surely leading this field. Some companies may even decide to just focus on the development and sale of RM. They will become pure RM vendors.

Today, the main procurement sources for RMs are:

- Software companies
- Consulting companies
- Industry organizations
- Academic organizations

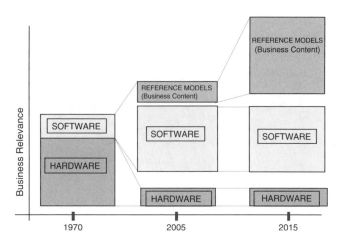

Fig. 6.4 Development of the IT market

Vendors of ERP systems were forced to make the business content of complex holistic software applications more transparent. For example, SAP documented the business processes enabled by their R/3 software in form of event-driven process chains (EPC) [5, 6]. Others, such as PeopleSoft (which has since been acquired by Oracle) followed. The software vendors, especially SAP, have been key drivers in the development of RM.

Consulting companies were also forced to structure their knowledge in the form of RM to increase their own productivity: They can use RMs to train consultants and make engagements more efficient and effective. RM provided by consulting companies can be especially interesting if the companies do not only include best practices but also next practices or suggestions for process innovations. Accenture's reference models, e.g., include not only process descriptions for 71 industries but also value-related components like capability assessment models KPI frameworks or value trees. These components enable an outcome-oriented use of the process reference models increasing the value of those models significantly. Using those models organizations can benefit from a vast industry-specific and cross-industry experience in a systematic efficient way. Especially, the use of RM from other industries to support emerging trends and "next practices" in the own industry has become a major trend and use case for RM. The models can typically be procured indirectly through consulting engagements. PMOLink is one company that already sells RM as products. They offer a RM for project management, based on the industry standard "PMBOK" [7]. To support usability, the RM is delivered in a database of the process-modeling system ARIS Platform [8]. The structure of the project management model is shown in Fig. 6.5. The size of this RM product is described in Fig. 6.6.

Industry organizations also deliver knowledge in the form of RM. For example, the Supply Chain Council offers the Supply Chain Operations Reference Model (SCOR) [9, 10]. SCOR is in its eighth version and has been continuously developed

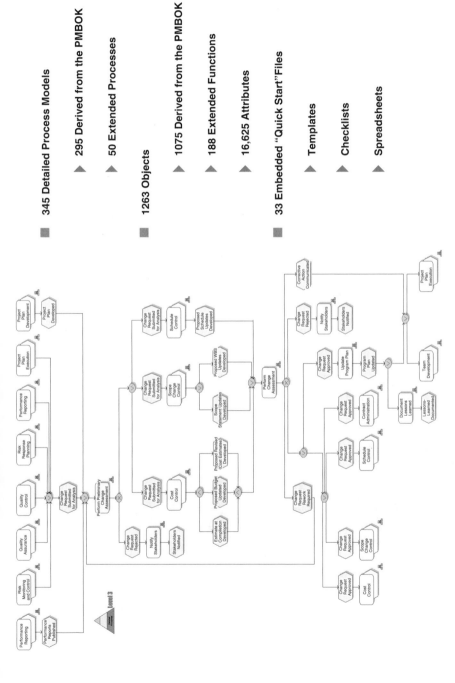

Fig. 6.5 Structure of PMOLink's project management reference model of PMOLink

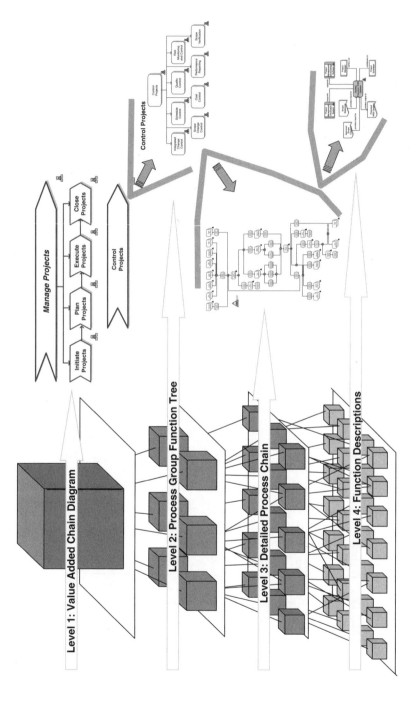

Fig. 6.6 Size of PMOLink's project management reference model

for more than 10 years. It is used all over the world and has received great recognition. It is a great example for a successful RM. Let us have a closer look at it.

SCOR is a business process reference model that contains all supply chain activities, from supplier's supplier to a customer's customer, including:

- All customer interactions, from order entry through paid invoice.
- All product (physical goods, services, etc.) transactions, including equipment, supplies, spare parts, bulk product, software, etc.
- All market interaction, from the understanding of the aggregate demand to the fulfillment of each order.

SCOR contains three levels of process detail. The top level (process types) defines the scope and content. It consists of the five top-level processes:

- Plan
- Source
- Make
- Deliver
- Return

The second level of SCOR, the configuration level (process categories), contains more than 30 process categories, such as "make to stock," "make to order," "engineer to order," or "production execution." These process categories can be used to "configure" a company's supply chain. Companies implement their operations strategy through the configuration they choose for their supply chain.

The third SCOR level, the process element level (decomposed processes), is used to fine-tune the operations of a company. It consists of the following:

- Process element definitions
- Process element information inputs and outputs
- Process performance metrics
- Best practices
- System capabilities necessary to support best practices
- Systems/tools to be used

Companies implement their supply chain solution on level 4 (or even more detailed levels). Level four, or the implementation level (decomposed subprocess), defines practices to achieve competitive advantage and to adapt to changing business conditions. This level is company specific and not in the scope of SCOR. The structure of SCOR is shown in Fig. 6.7.

The Value Chain Group is another industry organization that delivers an RM, the Value Reference Model (VRM). VRM focuses on the complete value chain with the top processes of plan, execute, and govern [11]. Also, the American Productivity and Quality Center (APQC) provides high-level reference models in form of industry-neutral and industry-specific frameworks [12]. These models are, e.g., used to structure processes for benchmarking purposes. RMs are great tools for industry organizations to organize the knowledge of their members and make it available in a useful format.

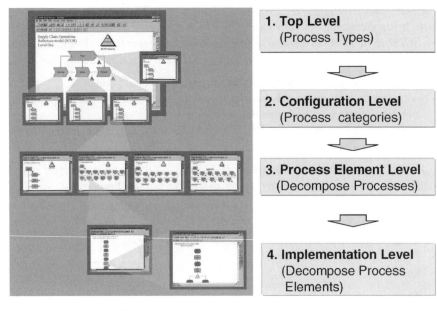

Fig. 6.7 Structure of SCOR

Academic organizations also deliver RM. Research in this area is popular in Europe, especially in Germany [4], but it is also evolving in other parts of the world. An example is Scheer's "Y-Model," a reference model for industrial enterprises [1, 13] that has been adapted to multiple industry sectors. The top level of the Y-Model for discrete manufacturing companies is shown in Fig. 6.8. The left side of the "Y" displays all order-related processes and the right side shows all product-focused processes. Horizontally, the "Y" structures the processes in execution and planning processes. The core support processes are defined above the "Y."

Becker's RM for retail enterprises [14, 15] is another example of an RM originating in academia. The RM, "retail-H," outlines various aspects of trade information systems, including contracting, order management, goods receipt, invoice auditing, accounts payable, warehousing, marketing, selling, goods issue, billing, and accounts receivable.

As the market for RM evolves, available models must be evaluated and compared. Just as one selects software, one also has to choose the appropriate RM. The following criteria can be used to support this RM selection process [16]:

- Syntactic criteria

    - Size
    - Correctness and consistency
    - Modularity
    - Structure (hierarchy)
    - Complexity

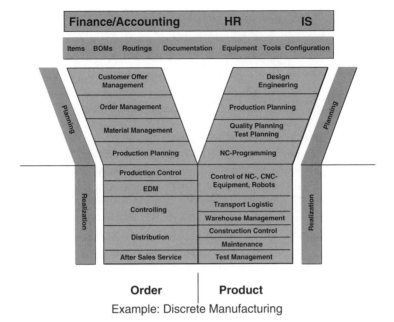

Fig. 6.8 "Y-Modei": reference model for industrial enterprises (after A.-W. Scheer)

- Architecture

- Semantic criteria

  - General applicability
  - Coverage of domain
  - Completeness
  - Efficiency of use
  - Expressiveness
  - Similarity with other models, possible overlaps
  - Comprehensibility
  - Documentation

- Pragmatic criteria

  - Popularity
  - Flexibility of use
  - Maturity
  - Relevance
  - Availability
  - Cost
  - Tool support

We have seen that RMs are already available on the market. We will now discuss how to apply an RM in a specific company situation to achieve the described benefits.

6.3   How Do You Apply RMs?

The basic procedure to apply RM to support business process design is fairly straightforward. Eliminate parts of the RM that are not relevant for your specific organization and adjust the process logic wherever necessary. If the RM is missing certain elements (e.g., a subprocess needed in your company), those elements are added to the model. The result is an enterprise-specific process model, as it has to be delivered in the process design of MPE through the process factory. This approach is visualized in Fig. 6.9.

The use of RM in the process design makes achieving process excellence easier. The above-described benefit leads in process initiatives to the following effects that are of great importance to enable an efficient and effective process design as required by MPE:

- Best and next practices are applied systematically
- A common terminology is used more or less automatically
- The design initiative remains business focused (also can be used to prepare for the implementation of IT, such as an ERP system)
- The scoping of a project is very effective (e.g., a process improvement initiative)
- The benchmarking with other organizations using similar basic structure is easier

Best and known "next" practices are not just used based on word of mouth, but on solid documentation. The RM defines the terminology to be used. This is especially important for work on inter-enterprise processes [10], in which members of multiple organizations are involved (e.g., a SCM improvement initiative), as discussed

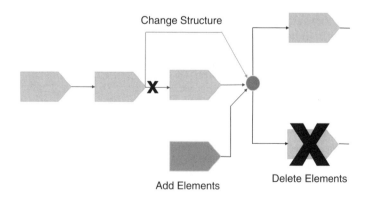

Fig. 6.9 Applying business process reference models

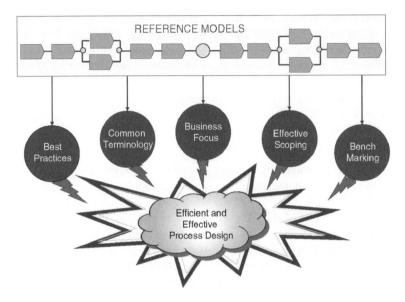

Fig. 6.10 Effects of the use of reference models

above. In such an environment, the RM ensures that everyone speaks the same language and uses terminology in the same manner. Software implementations, such as ERP projects, can be used to drive process improvements. However, project teams often lose focus on real business process topics. The use of RMs avoids that pitfall. An RM also supports the appropriate scoping of an initiative because it describes the relevant domain in a transparent way. Once several companies have organized their processes, based on the same RM, it becomes easier to benchmark the performance (e.g., the performance of supply chain processes can be compared using the structures delivered by Supply Chain Operations Reference Model (SCOR)). These effects of the use of RM are shown in Fig. 6.10.

RMs can be used for many company-specific initiatives and projects, including the following important applications [17, 18]:

- Business process design for a specific organization
- Validation of enterprise-specific models
- Development of standard software applications (could also be a company standard)
- Selecting software packages (e.g., ERP or services to be used in an SOA)
- Education and training

A challenge in applying RM is that the models generally do not include any information about what can be modified and how the modifications can look like, so that they really make sense. Is a specific subprocess of an RM optional or do I really need it? Does it make sense to change the sequence of certain functions? These are examples of questions that can be answered by RMs designed as configurable models [19]. These configurable RM deliver the following advantages [19]:

- Support decisions for the transformation of the model
- Configuration of all relevant aspects, including data or functions
- Configuration decisions are classified into mandatory and optional categories
- Configuration decisions are classified into global (central) and local decision categories
- Configuration decisions can be interrelated
- Relations of decisions must be transparent
- Guidelines for the use of the models
- Configurable models are very comprehensive

Although such configurable models are still not the norm, I am convinced that future RM products will increasingly reflect those requirements to expand the use of the models.

The application of RM is another core element of MPE. The process warehouse of the process factory contains all of an enterprise's relevant RM to be used in the company-specific design. This may also include industry models from various industries to exchange best practices across industry boundaries. For example, a biotechnology company may use the product configuration process developed for the machinery industry to organize the final configuration of their bio-substances to deliver the final products. RM enables the efficient and effective use of domain know-how around business process excellence.

6.4 The Bottom Line

- RMs are generic conceptual models, which formalize recommended practices for a special domain. This means RMs deliver best practice information that can be used many times (e.g., in multiple organizations). Their format enables easy application in specific situations (Sect. 6.1).
- RMs represent content of various domains, which can be used to distinguish various types of RM (Sect. 6.1).
- RMs provide key business benefits for process design, such as cost, time, and risk reduction or the improvement of the modeling quality (Sect. 6.1).
- The market for RM should increase significantly in the next few years, especially due to new, flexible SOA-based application software (Sect. 6.2).
- Today, the main procurement sources for RMs are software companies, consulting firms, industry organizations, and academic organizations (Sect. 6.2).
- Examples of available RM include the SAP RMs, the PMOLink project management model, the SCOR model, the VRM model, the Y-Model, and the retail-H model (Sect. 6.2).
- Criteria for the evaluation and selection of RM can be defined (Sect. 6.2).
- The basic procedure to apply RM to support business process design is fairly straightforward (Sect. 6.3).
- The use of RM in efficient and effective process design is required by MPE to enable high performance for the organization as a whole (Sect. 6.3).

- Configurable RMs facilitate the use and transformation of the RM into company-specific process models (Sect. 6.3).

References

1. Scheer, A W: Business Process Engineering – Reference Models of Industrial Enterprises, 2nd edn. Springer, Berlin (1994)
2. Fettke, P., Loos, P.: Classification of reference models.: A methodology and its application. Inf. Syst. E-Business Manag. **1**(1), 35–53 (2007)
3. Jost, W.: EDV-gestuetzte CIM Rahmenplanung. Gabler, Wiesbaden (1993)
4. Fettke, P, Loos, P: Perspectives on reference modeling. In: Fettke, P, Loos, P (eds.) Reference Modeling for Business Systems Analysis, pp. 1–20. Hershey, London (2007)
5. Kirchmer, M: Business Process Oriented Implementation of Standard Software – How to Achieve Competitive Advantage Efficiently and Effectively, 2nd edn. Springer, Berlin (1999)
6. Curran, T., Keller, G.: SAP R/3 business blueprint: Business engineering mit den R/3-Referenzprozessen. Bonn (1999)
7. PMOLink (ed.): Project Management Processes – Based on the PMBOK Guide. PMOLink, New Orleans (2004)
8. IDS Scheer AG (ed.): ARIS Platform. Product Brochure. Saarbruecken (2007)
9. Supply Chain Council (ed.): Supply Chain Operations Reference Model – Plan, Source, Make, Deliver, Return. Version 8.0 (2007)
10. Kirchmer, M, Brown, G, Heinzel, H: Using SCOR and other reference models for E-Business process networks. In: Scheer, A W, Abolhassan, F, Jost, W, Kirchmer, M (eds.) Business Process Excellence – ARIS in Practice, pp. 45–64. Springer, Berlin (2002)
11. Value Chain Group (ed.): Business Process Transformation Framework. In: www.value-chain.org (2007)
12. American Productivity and Quality Center (APQC): Business Process Frameworks. http://www.apqc.org/process-classification-framework (2011)
13. Scheer, A W, Jost, W, Guengoez, O: A reference model for industrial enterprises. In: Fettke, P, Loos, P (eds.) Reference Modeling for Business Systems Analysis, pp. 167–181. Hershey, London (1997)
14. Becker, J, Schuette, R: Handelsinformationssysteme, 2nd edn. Redline Wirtschaft, Frankfurt (2004)
15. Becker, J, Schuette, R: A reference model for retail enterprises. In: Fettke, P, Loos, P (eds.) Reference Modeling for Business Systems Analysis, pp. 182–205. Hershey, London (2007)
16. van Belle, J: Evaluation of selected enterprise reference models. In: Fettke, P, Loos, P (eds.) Reference Modeling for Business Systems Analysis, pp. 266–286. Hershey, London (2007)
17. Fettke, P, Loos, P: Reference models for retail enterprises. HMD Prax. Wirtschaftsinformatik **235**, 15–25 (2004)
18. Kirchmer, M, Scheer, A W: Change management – key for business process excellence. In: Scheer, A W, Abolhassan, R, Jost, W, Kirchmer, M (eds.) Business Process Change Management – ARIS in Practice, pp. 1–14. Springer, Berlin (2003)
19. Recker, J, Rosemann, M, van der Aalst, W, Jansen-Vullers, M, Drelling, A: Configurable reference modeling languages. In: Fettke, P, Loos, P (eds.) Reference Modeling for Business Systems Analysis, pp. 22–46. Hershey, London (2007)

Chapter 7
Inter-enterprise Business Processes Enabled by MPE

Although many organizations still focus on the design and implementation of their internal business processes to overcome functional barriers, an increasing number of companies are targeting the integration between enterprises, or so-called inter-enterprise processes. Successful companies must operate in a network with other organizations to leverage their strengths and compensate for their weaknesses. Mutual interdependencies are created and managed to drive additional value and to ensure high performance for the organization as a whole.

We previously discussed Dell, a company that focuses on its sales and supply chain capabilities. Third-party organizations manufacture the components of its PCs and other products. Thus, the company works in a collaboration network using intensively inter-enterprise processes.

These changing management paradigms are reflected in a changing information technology focus. The focus moves from integrated intra-enterprise application packages, such as ERP systems, to Internet-based "e-enabled" and inter-enterprise focused IT, using next-generation automation and integration approaches. Enabling IT environments, like SOA, becomes key and the Web plays a paramount role. This leads to "e-business processes" (i.e., inter-enterprise processes supported through Web-enabled technology). These processes have the ability to cross multiple organizations and require a well-suited approach for BPM [1–4]. Management of process excellence (MPE) fulfills the resulting requirements, related to an inter-enterprise environment, as well as to e-technologies.

This chapter will discuss tools and procedures for the design, implementation, execution, management, and controlling of inter-enterprise processes, empowered through the Web and SOA architectures. We will focus on specific inter-enterprise aspects, since we have already discussed the technology aspects. The approach describes how to build and manage collaborative business scenarios, enabled through the Internet, so-called e-business scenarios. All phases of MPE are involved in the discussion. This is visualized in Fig. 7.1.

M. Kirchmer, *High Performance Through Process Excellence*,
DOI 10.1007/978-3-642-21165-2_7, © Springer-Verlag Berlin Heidelberg 2011

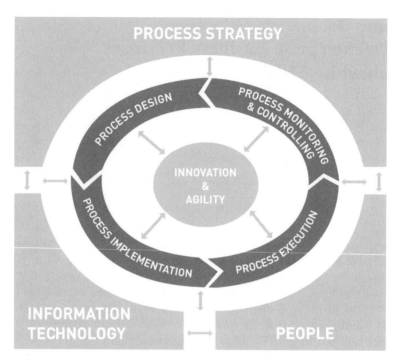

Fig. 7.1 Focus on all phases of MPE

7.1 What Are Inter-enterprise Processes and Why Are They Significant?

Inter-enterprise processes are business processes that are distributed across two or more organizations that are independent legal units; thus, there is generally no centralized control. Therefore, the organizational environment of the processes is even more heterogeneous than one of intra-enterprise processes across various organizational units of one company. This results in special integration and coordination requirements regarding people, as well as technology and aspects.

These requirements are constantly increasing because companies are more and more often forced to be part of several networks, and with that, participate in multiple inter-enterprise processes. The members of those processes are often dispersed around the globe, leading to additional challenges [2]. We will discuss the aspect of globalization in detail later and will now focus on the general inter-enterprise situation.

On the technology side, flexible SOA-based IT environments support inter-enterprise processes. They enabled the integration of heterogeneous IT, on the basis of capabilities of the Internet and related standards. This results in Internet-based processes that are often called e-business processes. The organizational integration must be organized through an appropriate BPM approach.

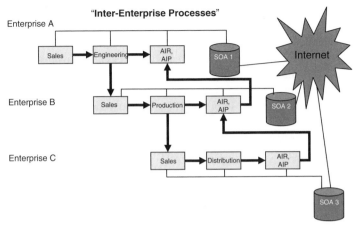

Fig. 7.2   Example of an inter-enterprise process

In most cases, an organization's integration in inter-enterprise processes allows the organization to focus on its core competencies, while benefiting from the key strengths of other organizations. For example, in an inter-enterprise scenario, one company may focus on the engineering activities, delivering world-class blueprints for machines. The second enterprise is a leading manufacturing company, producing the machines on the basis of the blueprint from its "supplier." The third organization is a logistics company that specializes in distribution activities. This company ensures the final delivery of the manufactured machine. Every company has one main core process, based on the specific offering. However, for the final customer who buys the machine, only the overall inter-enterprise process is relevant. If a customer receives the machine too late, he or she does not really care if the blueprint was not finished in time or if the production was delayed or if there were delivery problems. If the final customer is not satisfied, it is an issue for each company involved in the inter-enterprise process. It has to be seen and organized as one overall business processes. This inter-enterprise process is shown in Fig. 7.2.

Supply chain processes are often discussed as inter-enterprise processes. They integrate suppliers and customers within an overall process [5]. Collaborative engineering processes or maintenance processes are also examples. In general, various enterprise networks that form inter-enterprise processes can be distinguished [6] as:

- Vertical networks
- Horizontal networks
- Regional networks
- Out-of-necessity networks
- Self-promoted networks
- Other networks

Vertical networks more or less represent the classic supply chain: one company adds value to a product and passes it onto the next one in the network. In horizontal networks, the involved companies have the same core competencies and all share capacity (e.g., production capacity to avoid bottlenecks). Companies of one region may create a regional network to facilitate close collaboration. For example, this can allow several small organizations to combine their capabilities to fulfill larger orders or demonstrate greater stability. These regional networks are similar to the out-of-necessity networks. For example, if one company cannot pay necessary research and development (R&D) for a new product, it may conduct R&D in an inter-enterprise engineering process together with other organizations. A member of a self-promoted network is a company with a core competency that it wants to include in as many networks as possible, independent of the specific final product. Collection companies, e.g., may strive for inclusion in as many inter-enterprise processes as possible and, therefore, form a self-promoted network. All forms of enterprise networks and the resulting processes must be supported by an appropriate BPM approach.

The use of standards, such as best practices, also promotes inter-enterprise processes. For example, if many companies use the same industry standard, this process could be outsourced, resulting in inter-enterprise processes [7]. Therefore, the broad use of the previously discussed reference models supports the outsourcing of processes, and with that, the creation of inter-enterprise business processes.

The participation in enterprise networks and the related inter-enterprise business processes results in many advantages, such as [6]:

- Synergy effects from leveraging each member's strengths.
- Speed: You can react quickly to a change by adding a new company with new capabilities to the network.
- Flexibility: Change (e.g., offering products through a new partner or leveraging another partner's production capacities).
- Risk reduction: You share risks with other enterprises, reducing your own risk.
- Independence: You are not forced to integrate into a larger enterprise group.
- Faster growth and increased profits through the use of the aforementioned synergies.
- Lasting customers through the broad capabilities of the network.
- Less capital required through the use of mutual capabilities.
- Quick failure recognition and feedback: The relationships between the partners of an inter-enterprise process are open enough to provide prompt feedback.
- Increased ability to deal with change, due to speed and flexibility.
- However, an extensive collaboration in networks and the resulting inter-enterprise processes can also lead to disadvantages, including [6].
- Too much reliance on one partner in the network, and with that, dependence on the condition of this partner.
- Too much mutual dependence, so that individual survival (e.g., in case one partner resigns from the network) is no longer possible.
- Pressure resulting from excessive coordination requirements.

- Lack of overall agility and responsiveness to market changes due to detail cross-company planning.
- Exclusive arrangements between partners of an inter-enterprise process, slowing down innovation and agility.
- Failure to support a struggling partner of the processes in a timely manner.
- Risk of missing outsourcing opportunities for support and management processes.
- Ignoring alternative networks or processes.
- Too much or too little mutual trust.
- Neglecting other core competencies currently not present in the inter-enterprise process.

An appropriate BPM approach reduces those risks.

In general, the BPM approach discussed earlier, with its methods and tools, can also be used for inter-enterprise processes. The views of the ARIS architecture [8, 9], the basis of MPE, are also relevant for those processes across organizations. The application of the discussed structure of ARIS to business processes facilitates the handling of specifics of inter-enterprise processes.

The use of the Internet allows companies to change and extend their offerings. For example, instead of selling music CDs, companies can offer music file downloads directly from the Web, or packages in transit can be tracked through the Internet – as an additional customer service. Therefore, the examination of a specific "deliverable view" of business processes, as suggested by the ARIS Architecture, is extremely important for an e-business environment.

Inter-enterprise business processes enable the efficient and effective collaboration between enterprises. In other words, responsibilities are shared between organizational units of the collaborating enterprises. As a consequence, the examination, and sometimes the change, of organizational structures become key for the design and implementation of inter-enterprise processes. This is another aspect handled in a specific view of the ARIS architecture, the organization view.

The collaboration of different organizations leads to "process-to-process" integration [10]. The coordination of all aspects necessary to achieve this integration is handled as a key aspect in the control view of the ARIS architecture.

Inter-enterprise processes are subject to change even more over time. They are not only influenced through the environment of one company, but through changes relevant for a whole network of enterprises. Therefore, the continuous management and controlling of those processes is especially important and challenging. Inter-enterprise processes generally require the agility discussed earlier.

We have now identified key characteristics of inter-enterprise processes. But what does that mean for a BPM approach? How do those characteristics of inter-enterprise processes influence the design and implementation of business processes? How must the execution and controlling of processes be modified? What does MPE need to deliver to achieve the required performance to manage inter-enterprise processes?

7.2   What Does It All Mean for the Design and Implementation of Processes?

Is the design and implementation of such inter-enterprise process truly different? What has to be changed in comparison to the business processes within an organization? The design of such company networks with related inter-enterprise processes requires the examination of three key areas [11]:

- A company's business processes, including the current interaction with external players, such as customers, suppliers, or other partners
- The business proposition a company offers to its customers
- The degree of participation with other organizations in creating shared business processes, harmonized across the inter-enterprise environment

The differences between inter- and intra-enterprise initiatives begin with the definition of goals in the strategy and design phase of MPE. Contrary to pure intra-enterprise processes, the distribution of benefits between involved organizational units plays an important role. A company's business proposition must improve through the collaboration in an inter-enterprise process. Within one company, the investment of additional resources in one department can achieve advantages in other departments. In an inter-enterprise environment, however, the distribution of expected benefits between various involved organizations becomes an important aspect of the goal definition. All involved organizations should realize benefits. In the very least, the state of an organization should not end up inferior to what it was previously. Otherwise, the inter-enterprise initiative will not be accepted and the resulting process cannot be realized.

The goals can again be defined by using elements of the Balanced Scorecard (BSC) methodology [12]. The separate examination of customer and process perspectives to define related goals is important for an inter-enterprise environment. It allows each organization to formulate specific requirements. The distribution of benefits between the involved organizations may be considered a strategic success factor to be achieved.

The next important activity in preparing the process design is the definition and extension of an organization's market offerings, consistent with the defined goals. The definition of offerings (of products) includes all customer-relevant aspects of the following components:

- Physical goods
- Services
- Information
- Rights
- Others

To define the offerings of a company, one or several of the product components are involved and relate to one another. Each of the product components may consist of several customer-relevant subcomponents.

In an e-business inter-enterprise environment, new offerings are mainly created though the following measures:

- The replacement of goods or services through information (e.g., replacement of CDs with electronic files)
- The combination of different products and services from several companies to one new offering (e.g., offer transportation services from different companies through one new "transportation portal")
- The enhancement of existing offerings through new processes (e.g., books, accessible through a convenient Internet store, the custom configuration of products)
- Others (e.g., creating new "products," such as data about stickiness of customers within Web sites)

It is essential to create new value for the customer through inter-enterprise networks. Although this can and often does include cost effects, the main focus is on value creation. A crucial aspect is the development of new service processes around existing offerings, which often becomes an important competitive factor and drives inter-enterprise initiatives. The new offerings can be represented in product models [13, 14], supporting an analytic approach to the definition of offerings.

This step of the design of inter-enterprise processes drives innovation activities, as required by MPE. Business model and technology innovations are included in this and the following process design steps [15]. Business process innovation plays the key role. In many instances, inter-enterprise initiatives force organizations to process innovations.

Once the offerings are defined, the resulting market partners must be determined. Market partners are customers, suppliers, or other organizations involved in the delivery and creation of the outlined offerings. Existing market partners may be considered along with new partners, eventually resulting from requirements of the goal definition. Companies often consider alternative partners to reduce and avoid high dependencies on a single partner.

New partners, with new capabilities, can lead to "collaboration innovation," a special type of process innovation. For example, when Cadillac launched its first sports utility vehicle, the Escalade, the car was nothing special. However, through a smart collaboration with a telecommunications company, Cadillac could offer the On Star Service, a telecommunications-based interactive navigation and concierge service system. This was something really new, something interesting that attracted new customers.

While determining business partners, it is important to identify the specific strengths of the company and its possible partners, which may be used as outsourcing partners for processes outside of the company's own core competence. Outsourcing, especially offshore outsourcing, has become increasingly popular because of factors like cost pressure in the United States and many European countries, rapid decline of communication costs, improvement of Internet stability, high-quality service providers, access to highly qualified offshore people and first success cases [16].

The decision to outsource processes or subprocesses must be evaluated during this design of inter-enterprise processes, considering the specific company situation. This evaluation should include coordination and additional process management cost created through the outsourcing decision.

To achieve the maximum advantage of an inter-enterprise environment, it is essential to focus on core competencies while integrated in a network of partners, each of which brings its core expertise to the table [17]. However, as explained previously, the integration of partners with similar strengths can also make sense in certain situations (e.g., to increase flexibility of production capacities).

The relationship between the partners of an inter-enterprise network may consist of the exchange of one or several of the following objects:

- Products (goods, services, etc.)
- Information
- "Good will, trust, other personal relations
- Others (e.g., money)

In most cases, the relationship between two partners involves the exchange of several of the aforementioned objects.

Now, it must be determined how these market partners should be integrated into a collaborative inter-enterprise business process. There may be direct point-to-point integration or a "star integration" through existing or to-be-created, so-called "e-marketplaces. These e-marketplaces facilitate the business relations of its members, based on Internet technologies. The point-to-point integration generally results in an optimized implementation of one relation; the use of an e-marketplace typically ensures increased flexibility to switch among partners. Marketplaces may be industry specific, regional, and/or even focused on the needs of one company trying to optimize its partner network (private marketplace) [18–20]. The discovery of existing e-marketplaces may result in changes in the defined partner network: partners may be added or eliminated, ultimately resulting in the definition of the topology of the partner network.

When the offerings and the partner network topology are defined, the resulting inter-enterprise scenarios can be designed. That means different business processes across multiple organizations are specified. These inter-enterprise processes outline the collaboration between the involved organizations. General business strategies, like collaborative engineering or planning, are defined in this activity. The key here is the knowledge about the organization's current business processes, to know how much they need to change or where it is necessary to harmonize those processes across all partners of a network.

It is important to evaluate the related intra-enterprise processes. If they cannot keep up with the new inter-enterprise capabilities, the targeted results will not occur. On the contrary, the tight integration may reveal the organization's own weaknesses to the other members of the network. In most cases, some of the intra-enterprise processes must also be changed and adapted to the new inter-enterprise scenario.

Each organization plays a specific role in a specific scenario. The definition of these roles is another important step in the definition of the entire scenario.

This collaboration creates new added value for the customer in enabling the defined offerings. The definition of these inter-enterprise scenarios is a key deliverable of the MPE design phase. These scenarios are the guidelines for all additional activities. Partners may play roles as suppliers, buyers, facilitators, etc.

Related process reference models can be used as a starting point for the definition of such inter-enterprise scenarios. These reference models allow the structured transfer of best practices and experiences within specific business fields. In addition, they are used to establish standards across various organizations (e.g., a common terminology), enabling efficient and effective inter-enterprise processes.

On the basis of the general process scenarios, the detailed inter-enterprise processes can be specified. The analysis of the relevant existing processes ensures a realistic implementation strategy. Processes to be analyzed include inter-enterprise and intra-enterprise processes and subprocesses. Both must fit together to enable appropriate business results. However, a special focus is naturally on the processes or subprocesses responsible for the collaboration of the involved organizations.

Companies must decide on three groups of processes to come up with the optimal inter-enterprise processes in your collaboration scenario [11]:

• Processes you perform yourself – mainly intra-enterprise processes
• Processes you perform with others – mainly inter-enterprise processes
• Processes others perform for you ("outsourced processes"), resulting in new inter-enterprise relations

The grouping of processes is the basis for the assignment of responsibilities across enterprise boundaries. This can be a time-consuming process because all involved enterprises must reach a consensus. Some questions to support that task include [11] the following:

• Of all companies in an inter-enterprise network, which has the best capabilities to manage a process?
• How will the capabilities of the different organizations be used in the inter-enterprise process?
• Have the responsibilities in the processes been clearly assigned?
• How do we determine when one company is not performing sufficiently?

On the one hand, the analysis focuses on general business approaches, as defined in the inter-enterprise scenarios (e.g., Is a collaborative engineering approach already implemented or does it still have to be defined?). On the other hand, process inefficiencies are discovered and resolved through the inter-enterprise collaboration.

The "to-be" of the core business processes can be specified on the basis of the defined inter-enterprise scenarios. This includes the assignment of the various responsibilities. The specification contains all ARIS information systems views: organizations, functions, data, products, and control flow. The different views may be specified in an integrated representation or separately, depending on the complexity of the aspects to be specified. The previously discussed approach of the MPE process factory is applied in this instance.

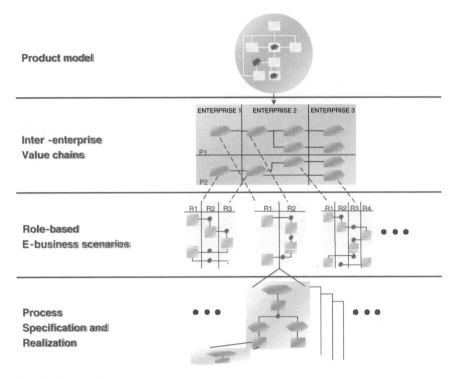

Fig. 7.3 Design of inter-enterprise processes

The structure of the design of inter-enterprise business processes is shown in Fig. 7.3.

On the basis of the business process specifications and the inter-enterprise scenarios, the required IT components can be selected. The focus here is on collaborative technologies, around SOA and the concept of Enterprise 2.0+, as discussed previously. In this stage, one may even find new online communities for the members of the inter-enterprise processes. This allows members to facilitate the collaboration using techniques, such as blogs or other means of joint content creation.

The process specification is the basis for the realization of the inter-enterprise scenarios, similar to the implementation of intra-enterprise processes. The business process models are used as a guideline for the implementation of the selected IT components. To ensure a fast, efficient, and effective implementation in an inter-enterprise environment, different subprocesses or functions are realized, according to the capabilities and priorities of the enterprises within the network. Because all individual activities refer to the integrated process design (a "master plan" for inter-enterprise scenarios), subprocesses are reassembled step by step to support end-to-end processes across the organization.

The specific realization activities vary greatly, depending on the environments of the involved companies. Therefore, it is impossible to describe all necessary activities in detail. However, a basic structure of the realization measures can be defined, similar to the realization of intra-enterprise processes [21]. The major steps are:

1. IT-related activities
2. Organizational activities
3. Go live

Contrary to pure intra-enterprise processes, the IT measures of an inter-enterprise process implementation may include more integration work (e.g., the use of additional enterprise application integration software, due to heterogeneous IT components of the involved enterprises, if an entire SOA environment is not available).

Also, the configuration and software development activities within inter-enterprise initiatives may relate closely to business initiatives, especially marketing and legal activities. For example, the development of Web pages requires a design based on marketing requirements. The exchange of specific information may also be defined by legal contracts and specifications.

On the basis of organizational measures, personnel, process organization, and general infrastructure-related activities can be distinguished. Personnel measures include all change management activities, especially training, but also information and communication, as discussed earlier. These change management activities are all conducted, based on the business process models developed in the design phase of MPE. With regard to process organization-related measures, legal or security aspects of inter-enterprise processes must be resolved.

Once IT and organizational measures are executed, the specified business processes can "go live," based on the new IT and organizational infrastructure. In other words, the process will change according to the design of the inter-enterprise scenarios. This requires appropriate support from the involved organizational units, similar to intra-enterprise projects.

The inter-enterprise processes are now ready to be executed and managed. So how do the specifics of the inter-enterprise environment influence those phases of MPE?

7.3   What Does It All Mean for the Execution and Controlling of Processes?

The implementation phase begins the process execution, which then requires the management and controlling of the inter-enterprise processes, as explained in the general discussion of MPE. Continuous process improvement must begin immediately to ensure that the targeted goals are actually achieved and to adapt to changing environments. Because of the higher rate of change, this is even more important in an inter-enterprise environment. Therefore, the current business situation has to be monitored constantly and compared with the design results. It must be determined whether the defined goals are achieved. If they are not achieved, either smaller improvement steps may be defined and executed (in a "Kaizen" approach of continuous improvement in smaller steps [22]) or a new strategy or design phase must begin to react to a drastically altered environment [23].

In an inter-enterprise environment, the major challenge of this activity is that one company generally cannot make that decision alone. It often requires lengthy discussions between members of the involved organizations. This issue can be alleviated if clear responsibilities are defined in the design phase. In many cases, there is one "dominating" partner in such an inter-enterprise network. This company can drive the necessary decisions. This situation often occurs in the automotive industry, but also in other industry sectors (e.g., in the retail area).

To monitor and analyze inter-enterprise business processes means to collect business process performance data and check if the defined goals have been realized, based on the newly implemented processes. Once again, it is most efficient to focus on core processes because they are most relevant for achieving business goals. The analysis determines whether or not the goals are realized. If the goals are not realized, the reasons must be determined (e.g., inconsistencies between an actual process and the relevant design of the specification phase). In addition, the business environment has to be continuously monitored for new developments (new products, competitors, business models, technologies, etc.) that may change the basis upon which the inter-enterprise design had been developed.

The collection and analysis of the relevant data is generally very time and work consuming. To execute this step efficiently and effectively, appropriate software tools play a key role. The manual execution of this step must basically be replaced by an application software system. One example of a tool focused on this process performance monitoring is the ARIS Process Performance Manager of the ARIS Platform [24]. It can be integrated with application software to collect the necessary process performance data (e.g., concerning cycle times).

Such a process management system can be used specifically to monitor inter-enterprise business processes, as shown in Fig. 7.4. In this case, it is recommended that a third-party service provider host the process management application to ensure that no confidential data are transferred between the involved organizations. This would be part of a process outsourcing product offered on the market.

In addition, the general business environment must be continuously evaluated. This can be achieved through the integration of external information sources, as explained previously in the discussion of the Enterprise 2.0+. Membership in various business online communities or the integration of research institutions in the "virtual organization" created through inter-enterprise processes can help to resolve this situation.

Because the governance of those inter-enterprise processes is challenging, it is recommended to document the key governance rules again in process models, so the governance processes can be managed effectively. The MPE approach can be applied to those governance processes. An example of such a process is the reaction to certain changes in the business environment, synchronized across all organizations of an inter-enterprise network.

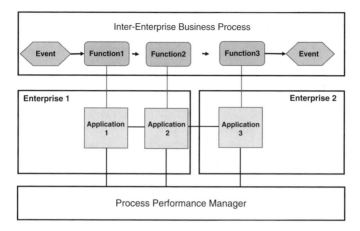

Fig. 7.4 Process performance management applied to inter-enterprise processes

Communication between the people involved in the process must also be organized, and it is best to include face-to-face meetings. This is necessary to bridge various cultural environments in the companies involved in inter-enterprise processes.

The general approach and philosophy of MPE also fits the requirements of inter-enterprise processes. However, specific design steps are necessary. During the execution of inter-enterprise processes, the overall controlling must be organized carefully.

7.4   Bottom Line

- Inter-enterprise processes are business processes that are distributed across two or more organizations that are independent legal units (Sect. 7.1).
- Inter-enterprise processes require special integration and coordination activities in regards to people, as well as technology, aspects as part of Management of Process Excellence if they are to enable high performance (Sect. 7.1).
- On the technology side, flexible SOA-based IT environments support those inter-enterprise processes. The organizational integration must be organized through an appropriate BPM approach (Sect. 7.1).
- In most cases, an organization's integration in inter-enterprise processes allows the organization to focus on its core competencies, while benefiting from key strengths of other organizations (Sect. 7.1).
- An extensive collaboration in networks and the resulting inter-enterprise processes can also lead to disadvantages (Sect. 7.1).
- Inter-enterprise processes are even more subject to change over time (Sect. 7.1).
- Contrary to pure intra-enterprise processes, the distribution of benefits between involved organizational units plays an important role (Sect. 7.2).

- An important activity to prepare the process design is the definition and extension of an organization's market offerings. The design of inter-enterprise processes drives innovation activities, especially process innovation (Sect. 7.2).
- New partners in inter-enterprise processes can lead to "collaboration innovation," a special form of process innovation (Sect. 7.2).
- Inter-enterprise scenarios, or different business processes across multiple organizations, are specified. It is important to evaluate and, if necessary, adjust the related intra-enterprise processes (Sect. 7.2).
- Each organization of an enterprise network plays a specific role in a specific scenario. The definition of these roles is very important for the definition of the entire scenario (Sect. 7.2).
- Responsibilities must be clearly assigned to the different partners of an enterprise network (Sect. 7.2).
- The specific realization activities for inter-enterprise processes vary heavily, depending on the specific situations in the various organizations involved (Sect. 7.2).
- A continuous process improvement must begin immediately after the "go live" to ensure that the targeted goals are actually achieved and to adapt to changing environments. Because of the higher rate of change, this is even more important in an inter-enterprise environment than for intra-enterprise processes (Sect. 7.3).
- The major challenge of continuous improvement activities in an inter-enterprise environment is that there is generally not one company who can make the necessary decisions, so third-party service providers may be used (e.g., for data collection) (Sect. 7.3).
- Collaboration technologies, as used in the Enterprise 2.0, can be very useful to coordinate inter-enterprise processes (Sect. 7.3).
- Since the governance of those inter-enterprise processes is challenging, it is recommended to document the key governance rules again in process models (Sect. 7.3).

References

1. Kirchmer, M: e-Business process improvement (eBPI): Building and managing collaborative e-Business scenarios. In: Callaos, N, Loutfi, M, Justan, M (eds.) Proceedings of the 6th World Multiconference on Systemics, Cybernetics and Informatics, vol. VIII, pp. 387–396. International Institute of Informatics and Systemics, Orlando (2002)
2. Fingar, P: Extreme Competition – Innovation and the Great 21st Century Business Reformation. Meghan-Kiffer Press, Tampa (2006)
3. Scheer, A-W, Habermann, E, Koeppen, A: Electronic Business und Knowledge Management – Neue Dimensionen fuer den Unternehmenserfolg. In: Scheer, A-W (ed.) Electronic Business und Knowledge Management – Neue Dimensionen fuer den Unternehmenserfolg, pp. 3–36. Physica Verlag, Heidelberg (1999)
4. Hammer, M.: The internet and the real economy. Documentation of Sapphire 99, Philadelphia (1999)

5. Kirchmer, M: E-business process networks – successful value chains through standards. J. Enterp. Manage. **17**(1), 20–30 (2004)
6. McHugh, P, Merli, G, Wheeler, W: Beyond Business Process Reengineering – Towards the Holistic Enterprise. Wiley, Chichester/New York (1995)
7. Davenport, T: The coming commoditization of processes. Harvard Business Review **83**(6), 100–108 (2005)
8. Scheer, A-W: ARIS – Business Process Frameworks, 2nd edn. Springer, Berlin/New York/Others (1998)
9. Scheer, A-W: ARIS – Business Process Modeling, 2nd edn. Springer, Berlin/New York/Others (1998)
10. Reilly, B., Hope-Ross, D., Knight, L.: Marketplaces and process mediation – The missing link. In: Gartner Group (ed.): Research Note, COM-11-6855, 19 Sept 2000
11. Champy, J: X-Engineering the Corporation – Reinventing Your Business in the Digital Age. Warner Books, New York (2002)
12. Kaplan, R S, Norton, D P: The Balanced Scorecard. Harvard Business School Press, Boston (1996)
13. Kirchmer, M: Market- and product-oriented definition of business processes. In: Elzina, D J, Gulledge, T R, Lee, C Y (eds.) Business Engineering, pp. 131–144. Kluwer, Norwell (1999)
14. Kirchmer, M, Enginalev, A: Internationales Informations-management – Aufbau von Informationssystemen im Internationalen Verbund. In: Zentes, J, Swoboda, B (eds.) Fallstudien zum Internationalen Management, pp. 717–729. Gabler, Wiesbaden (2000)
15. Davila, T, Epstein, M J, Shelton, R: Making Innovation Work. Wharton School Publisher, Upper Saddle River (2006)
16. Robinson, M, Kalakota, R: Offshore Outsourcing – Business Models, ROI and Best Practices. Mivar Press, Alpharetta (2004)
17. Kalakota, R., Robinson, M.: e-Business – Roadmap for Success. Berkeley/Others (1999)
18. Williams, L.: E-MarketOS: how BtoB marketplaces are creating a commerce operating system. In: The Yankee Group (ed.) BtoB Commerce & Applications Report, Vol. 5, No. 11, The Yankee Group, Boston (June 2000)
19. Williams, L.: Corporate-sponsored vs. independent BtoB exchanges: who will win? In: The Yankee Group (ed.) BtoB Commerce & Applications Report, Vol. 5, No. 12, The Yankee Group, Boston (July 2000)
20. Runyan, G.: Logistics marketplaces: shaping the evolution of BtoB commerce. In: The Yankee Group (ed.) BtoB Commerce & Applications Report, Vol. 5, No. 13, The Yankee Group, Boston (July 2000)
21. Kirchmer, M: Business Process Oriented Implementation of Standard Software: How to Achieve Competitive Advantage Efficiently and Effectively, 2nd edn. Springer, Berlin/New York/Others (1999)
22. Imai, M.: Kaizen – Der Schluessel zum Erfolg der Japaner im Wettbewerb, 8 Auflage. Muenchen (1993)
23. Nolan, T, Goodstein, L, Pfeiffer, J W: Plan or Die! 10 Keys to Organizational Success. Pfeiffer, San Diego (1993)
24. IDS Scheer A.G. (ed.): ARIS Platform. Product Brochure. Saarbruecken (2007)

Chapter 8
Emergent Processes Enabled by MPE

Knowledge and the people who work with knowledge have become increasingly important for achieving high performance in today's business environment. Knowledge workers are people who "think for a living" [1] or, as Davenport, a business process and knowledge management thought leader, defines more precisely, people with a high degree of expertise, education, or experience. The primary purpose of their job involves the creation, distribution, or application of knowledge. Key areas where such knowledge workers are deployed include [1] the following:

- Management
- Business or financial operations
- Computers and mathematics
- Architecture and engineering
- Life, physical, and social sciences
- Legal
- Health care practices
- Community and social services
- Education, training, and library
- Arts, design, entertainment, sports, and media

Knowledge work is different than other types of work, mainly due to the fact that this type of work is generally less structured. It is typically not very easy to define a process model that describes knowledge work, as we discussed for the design phase of MPE. Special characteristics of knowledge work are [1]:

- Knowledge workers prefer autonomy
- A detailed specification of knowledge-intensive processes is less valuable and more difficult to define than other types of work
- You can observe a great deal about knowledge work by just watching it
- Knowledge workers generally have good reasons for their actions
- Commitment matters tremendously
- Knowledge workers value their knowledge and would not share it easily

M. Kirchmer, *High Performance Through Process Excellence*,
DOI 10.1007/978-3-642-21165-2_8, © Springer-Verlag Berlin Heidelberg 2011

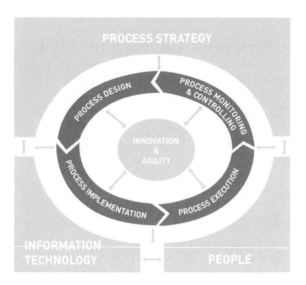

Fig. 8.1 Focus on all phases of MPE

Many knowledge-intensive processes, such as those within R&D environments or the management of large projects, cannot be completely defined upfront. These are emergent processes. Design and execution overlap heavily. Design results are based on the execution of preceding activities of the process. The importance of emergent processes continuously increases for many enterprises; however, their management is typically not addressed with straightforward business process management (BPM) approaches. Therefore, Majchrzak, Logan, McCurdy, and I conducted research on the management of those emergent processes [2, 3], focusing on defining working approaches and guidelines. This chapter is based on the results of our research.

The chapter focuses again on all phases of management of process excellence (MPE), explaining how it enables the management of emergent processes around the process life cycle. The focus of this chapter is visualized in Fig. 8.1.

The dominating resources needed for this approach are people, especially managers who apply MPE guidelines for managing emergent processes. Therefore, most of the topics discussed result in suggestions for those managers, rather than the infrastructure needed. However, the flexible and collaboration-based IT architectures, as used in the Enterprise 2.0+, are also very useful for the management of emergent processes.

8.1 What Are Emergent Processes and Why Are They Managed Differently?

Emergent business processes are knowledge-intensive processes for which the outcomes are unpredictable; participants must continuously make sense of their situation and decide, in real time, on the next steps to take. Thus, there is a high

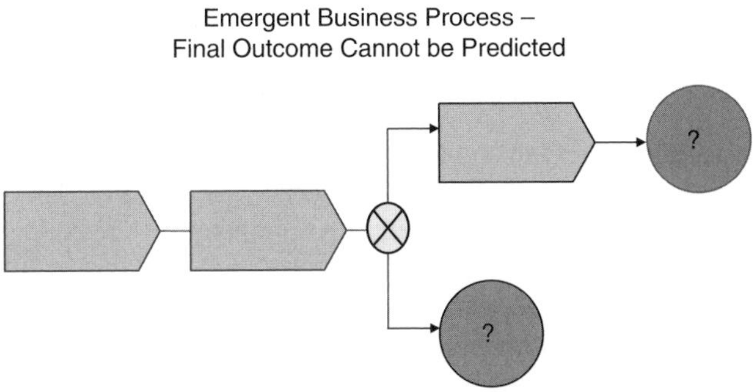

Emergent Business Process –
Final Outcome Cannot be Predicted

Fig. 8.2 Definition of emergent business processes

overlap between the phases of MPE: design, implementation, execution, and controlling of processes are only partly finished when triggering the following phase of the process life cycle. For example, if the first steps of the process are defined, they are directly implemented, executed, and checked before the next steps are designed. This definition of emergent processes is visualized in Fig. 8.2.

New product development, customer service, or any knowledge process conducted in a highly dynamic, competitive marketplace must be emergent if a company is to use the unpredictability of the environment for its competitive advantage. Emergence also happens when least expected. The Red Cross, Wal-Mart, and FedEx, responding to the Hurricane Katrina aftermath, worked together – in an unplanned way – to coordinate the delivery of bottled water to hurricane victims sooner and to more victims than other organizations, such as the City of New Orleans and local churches. Research has repeatedly demonstrated that managers contribute to a company's bottom line when they are able to support their employees in effectively handling unpredictability in the workplace and marketplace – and by so doing turn routine business and work processes into emergent ones.

Although managing emergence has been discussed to a great extent, the current literature provides managers with insufficient guidance about activities to undertake while their employees are dealing with the emergence (i.e., the process for managing emergence as it is happening). MPE supports that process of managing emergence.

Most of the existing advice focuses on enterprises establishing general policies for encouraging effective improvisation by workers responsible for emergent work processes:

- Contingency plans must be prepared
- Alternative future scenarios must be developed
- The right people must be brought into the workforce
- The environment must be closely monitored
- Reward structures encouraging experimentation must be established

The general activities supporting emergence are clearly critical. But, just as critical – yet much less examined – is what managers should do while workers carry out their emergent processes. Some questions exploring this topic include:

- Should managers step back and simply enforce the infrastructure?
- Should they continue to encourage their workers to improvise?
- Should they roll up their sleeves and send out experimental probes themselves?

Although it is most likely that managers need to do all three, they also need to do more if their companies are to manage emergence successfully. They must adapt management behavior to the environment, becoming part of the emergent business process.

Collectively, Majchrzak, Logan, McCurdy, and I have spent years managing companies and initiatives facing highly uncertain environmental and competitive pressures; leading, listening, and playing in jazz bands; and studying managers who we consider masters at managing emergence. Our collective experiences have led us to the conclusion that to successfully manage emergence, managers must be actively engaged in the emergent process itself – not simply offer encouragement or ensure that the infrastructure is working. However, if they just take control from employees and conduct the probes themselves, only confident, empowered workers will successfully adapt their processes and knowledge to unpredictable events. Instead, successful managers of emergent processes have their own work process that is unique to managing emergent processes. The work process and patterns are not the same for managing employees who are performing routine work.

Successful managers of emergent processes engage in the work process of streaming together "participatory innovative spurts." "Innovative spurts" are the ways in which people continuously innovate in how they do their work. This is a perfect fit with MPE. An engineer who reframes a problem from building a bridge to affecting the flow of traffic is engaged in an innovative spurt. The Red Cross's redirection during the Katrina disaster from a direct service delivery model to an information broker role is another example of an innovative spurt. In uncertain times, innovative spurts are needed because plans have broken down.

"Participatory" means that anyone may and should be able to take part in these innovative spurts, not simply those who are explicitly tasked with the responsibility to innovate. Subcontractors, customers, insiders, pundits – all can become engaged in innovative spurts. In the Katrina disaster, individuals and church groups independently posted names of missing persons. None had been tasked with the "responsibility" to find missing persons.

Finally, "streaming spurts together" means that instead of coordinating these spurts in a planned, top-down fashion, managers encourage and guide these innovative spurts to build on one another as they evolve. As Web sites and databases listing missing persons from Hurricane Katrina proliferated, the Red Cross stepped in to knit the sites together through links and a search engine – not centralizing the work of others, but rather to innovatively build on the spurts of others.

But how does one implement those "participatory innovative spurts"? How can one really manage such emergent processes?

8.2   How Can One Manage Emergent Processes?

To stream together participatory innovative spurts, four key management activities are necessary:

- Continuously engage in discourse with participants and encourage communication
- Dynamically update knowledge maps to continuously rematch participant responsibilities in a knowledge network
- Purposely blur boundaries between who is inside and outside the organization
- Govern through egocentric reputation networks and changing leadership, not rules

These guidelines for the management of emergent processes are visualized in Fig. 8.3.

What does it mean to engage in continuous discourse with potential participants? In the face of uncertain events, different perspectives are needed to solicit and evaluate alternative interpretations of events, information, and possible solutions. Typically, managers trying to cope with uncertainty will ask employees and consultants to develop white papers, top-down road maps, or market trend reports that are discussed and then used to form the basis for plans to guide employee behaviors. Managing emergence is more than that. Managers may solicit different views in the form of reports and employees may discuss these reports. However, the discussions do not end in a plan; in fact, the discussions do not end at all. The managers structure the work so that the discussion continues as the work is complete.

It is not just continuous discussion that is encouraged, but "discourse." Discourse is a discussion in which information, assumptions, and interpretations are

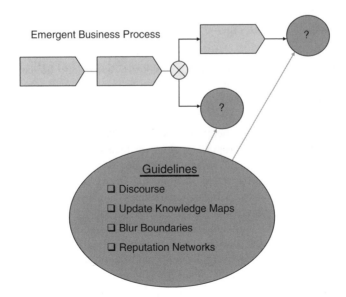

Fig. 8.3 Managing emergent business processes

explicitly surfaced, compared with other interpretations and then challenged in the face of new information and interpretations. Discourse for emergence is the constant sharing and challenging of assumptions about the environment, uncertainties, and possible organizational responses. Why would a manager encourage discourse during work hours even after decisions are made? In uncertain times, environmental realities change so rapidly and potentially with such systemic effects that interpretation and assumptions need to be surfaced and challenged frequently to identify the next innovative spurt. Because the business relevant change is continuously happening, the evaluation of potential next steps of emergent processes has to be reconsidered continuously.

Successful discourse is not the normal conversation of an everyday organization. It is different in three ways. First, for discourses to successfully lead to innovative spurts, participants must be able to freely share and discuss all relevant information, including taboo subjects such as political implications of alternative actions. Common performance metrics for each business unit can help by visibly conveying information on each unit's performance via dashboards, which are then openly discussed. Second, discourses must intentionally engage alternative perspectives, as when people from many different levels in an organization are engaged in a discourse. Third, discourses must be focused on actions. Discourses that lead to a lot of pontification will be of limited value; they must affect people's behaviors. In spite of all of the change, we have to move continuously toward an organization's goal. Emergent processes must be developed according to that requirement.

So, applying MPE for managing emergence means stimulating discourse by walking among workers and asking them questions like the following:

- Have any assumptions changed lately?
- Are you still sure this is the right thing to do?
- Have you thought about other actions we could be taking?

In the discourse, managers purposely include people who have been ignored previously. They share information that might be traditionally hidden. They talk about alternative actions people can take. For example, Novell managers use a process called "dialogic inquiry," in which participants air, openly challenge, and then discuss core assumptions they each hold. Managers have broken from tradition by no longer starting meetings between Novell consultants and software developers with participants presenting proposed actions or decisions. Instead, they begin the meeting with each participant presenting his/her assumptions about emerging market needs and corporate direction. Dialogic inquiry has worked to inspire innovative spurts in both product ideas and marketing campaigns, and contributed to a general sense of community and shared understanding.

Dynamically updating knowledge maps to continuously rematch responsibilities means the following: in changing and uncertain times, the knowledge that constituted relevant expertise given a certain set of known conditions may quickly become preempted by new knowledge as those conditions change. The notion of an "expert" is fleeting, highly situation specific, and of limited utility. It is not that people are not experts for a given problem or solution; it is that the set of known conditions continuously redefine what the problem is, and thus, the appropriate solutions and expertise. Expertise is then grounded in the knowledge that can be brought to bear on an issue as it is discussed.

Thus, MPE managers of emergence do not rely on static expertise directories, yellow pages, or their informal networks of contacts to determine who knows what about something. Instead, they develop – and help others to develop – knowledge maps about what people know about all sorts of unrelated topics and strive to keep these maps updated. Some managers do this by wandering around asking employees about hobbies. This is more than showing an interest in an employee; the hobbies, such as a fascination with Chinese history, may prove helpful in some future Chinese outsourcing deal. Managers may keep knowledge maps updated by sending out e-mails to employees with links to articles about new ways of doing business to see who starts a conversation about the article. Other managers observe posts to corporate blogs to see who is interested in what. They use the concept of the discussed Enterprise 2.0+ and its collaboration capabilities around Web 2.0 applications.

Having adopted the notion of keeping knowledge maps updated to rematch responsibilities, managers of emergence realize that personally updating the knowledge maps for their organization and shifting responsibilities on the fly is too slow for an emergent process. So they create and manage a process in which the workers responsible for the emergent process are able to keep knowledge maps updated to dynamically reshift responsibilities.

In the following true example, Rob and Paul are managers at the New Orleans public utility Entergy. Rob and Paul were responsible for placing the largest transmission cables ever built under the mile-wide Mississippi River. They completed the project on time and below budget. To accomplish this very involved project, Rob and Paul had to rely on contractors to handle each phase of the project – from dirt removal to cable manufacturing, from cable laying to building a shoreline children's park when construction was complete. Because of the size, novelty, and complexity of the project, Rob and Paul knew they would not be able to predefine all of the conditions for handoffs between contractors. So, they created a contractual arrangement in which each contractor was responsible for an effective handoff to the next contractor without specifying details of the handoff. The contractual arrangement effectively encouraged contractors to share their expertise about the site as it evolved with the changing conditions at the site, such as the evolving compaction of the dirt or unexpected underwater hazards. Contractors would negotiate responsibilities on the fly for solving problems as they learned from each other because they were both required to agree that a successful handoff had been completed before payment. In this way, Rob and Paul made it possible for the contractors to do their own knowledge map updating and responsibility shifting.

Purposely blurring boundaries between who is in and outside the organization results in the following behavior: Today, customers are often asked for feedback on product innovations. They are asked to suggest product ideas, to provide financial forecasts, product demand forecasts, and to partner with companies on developing process and product innovations. This behavior puts the company in the center of the communication network and customers have often been willing to offer help when asked. Managing emergence, however, requires more. Getting solicited feedback from customers is too slow and predictable for an emergent process. Moreover, keeping the company in the center of the communication network means that information will be lost unless it is explicitly routed through the company. Instead, emergent processes require unpredictable input from unpredictable participants.

Suppliers, interested citizens, and employees – as well as customers – need to become involved. The information they provide should not just be feedback in response to specific requests, but unsolicited information offered out of interest and excitement to become engaged. Ideally, such individuals are not only providing information, but helping to correct inaccurate information offered by others. When someone assumes a constraint on an idea, companies need customers, suppliers, and interested parties to challenge these constraints. Normally, such engagement would be expected only of employees. But emergent work processes cannot afford to miss information from outside the organization. So, managers of emergence blur the boundaries between what company employees do and what external parties do.

Novell has effectively blurred this distinction in its "Birds of a Feather" Forums. At corporate events for its customers, senior developers were traditionally kept out of the customer limelight because marketing employees, not developers, worked with the customer. But this approach changed with the Birds of a Feather Forums. Customers at these events now share their interests and questions about new products or new approaches for existing products. A senior developer with deep knowledge about the specific topic attends the event and discusses the subject matter with the customers, employees, media, and other interested parties. Although some developers may comment on future development activities that are not quite ready for public discussion, the open knowledge-sharing exchange has created relationships and innovative spurts that have inspired both sides.

Paul and Rob at Entergy, as employees of a public utility, knew that the public needed to be informed about the public works project if its cost was to be borne by rate increases, rather than Entergy. However, Paul and Rob went beyond simply informing the public; they engaged the public in weekly talk shows, town hall meetings, letters to the editor in the local newspapers, responses to others' letters to the editor, and open houses, at which they did not simply present, but used the time to solicit ideas, discuss unfolding problems in the project and involve the public in celebrations as the project went through its various phases. This level of customer engagement left the public feeling that they were not simply informed, but that they had influenced "their project." The public voted to grant the rate increase.

Another example is the increasing use of Enterprise 2.0+ concepts, such as wikis, to encourage engagement at all levels inside and outside an organization. At Novell, the Cool Solutions wiki invites customers to provide solutions for other customers, help developers to understand technical issues, and even cowrite technical white papers with Novell developers.

In the past, managers have been reluctant to share the details of an emergent process with outsiders for fear that others will conclude that the organization is rudderless, blowing in the wind of change. Public projects selectively release information to the public; developers selectively meet with only hand-picked customers; information is gathered from customers but interpreted by the organization behind the firewall. Engaging the external base of interested citizens not by simply providing information, but in helping to interpret the information is a level of responsibility given to external parties that blurs the boundaries between internal and external agents.

Govern through dynamic, egocentric reputation networks, not rules. If managers of emergent processes need innovation spurts not only from employees but also external parties, what leverage do managers have to make this happen? The MPE managers of emergence understand that rules ensure that people will follow rules, but rules will not ensure that people participate in innovate. Instead, managers have created or identified "reputation networks" and used these networks to provide the incentives and the norms for participatory innovation.

Governing by reputation has been found to be useful in the past. Wiki pages indicate the contributor with the greatest number of downloaded pages. Knowledge management systems enable people to rate each others' contributions in terms of how the contribution helps with their immediate problem. EBay rates sellers and buyers. Southern California Edison's Web governance structure for its employee portal governs by reputation. The owners of each port of the portal are publicly known, creating a sort of "United Nations" effort at portal management. The result is a portal that is well managed and kept up to date, in part because reputations are on the line.

However, it's not simply the reputation of individual people that matters if participatory innovation spurts are desired in response to uncertain events. In managing emergence, because problems and events change unpredictably and dynamically, a reputation network for uncertain times is also likely to be dynamic. Thus, instead of a network as a stable community that doles out reputation kudos, a reputation network for emergent processes would be highly unique for each individual party, and uniquely adjusted by that party in response to each unique event.

For example, rather than use a general network of security professionals, chief security officers typically selectively draw from their own personal networks to recreate an unique reputation network for each unique security threat they encounter. Therefore, using these networks for governing requires first identifying them. Then, having identified those networks, the MPE managers work with the network to affect how reputation within the network is assigned.

For example, Rob and Paul at Entergy knew that they did not have enough leverage to keep their subcontractors on track. So, they learned about the market communities within which each subcontractor worked and then publicly kept that community informed about the subcontractor's progress. In one case, Rob flew to Japan to speak to the subcontractor's customers to explain why working on this subcontract would yield long-term dividends to the customers – a move that gave the subcontractor flexibility to innovatively reschedule production when he encountered problems with the Entergy project.

These four guidelines help managers of emergent processes to react quickly to the uncertainty in unpredictable events – so quickly that it appears from the outside that they are preemptive strategists, prescient soothsayers, excellent predictors of the future, and great planners. Nothing could be further from the truth. What sets them apart from others is neither their planning skills nor their ability to look through a crystal ball. What sets them apart is their continuous discourse, updating knowledge maps, blurring organizational boundaries, and using reputations within egocentric networks among an ever-changing group of participants. By streaming together the participatory innovative spurts that result, managers are able to make an emergent process appear expected.

Although this management behavior is crucial, a certain infrastructure is still necessary. We will now discuss the tools supporting the management of emergent business processes.

8.3   What Tools Support the Management of Emergent Processes?

In our discussion of general guidelines for managing emergent business processes, it was determined that the concept of the Enterprise 2.0+ helps to implement and enable the application of those guidelines. Wikis or blogs are used to collect and exchange knowledge in an efficient and effective way. They support the knowledge worker, especially in the described environment of emergence. The support of an internal and external collaboration through Web 2.0 applications, such as online communities, facilitates all four discussed guidelines. It helps blurring company boundaries, creating external networks, defining knowledge maps, and can even enable the required discourse.

The components of an Enterprise 2.0+ environment can be combined with a telecommunications environment supporting the necessary intense communication. Certain events may trigger phone calls to cellular phones or start in parallel an "ad hoc blog" related to the same topic. The intense discourse is channeled through various media, bridging even long distances where necessary.

The continuous update and management of knowledge maps can be supported by BPM applications, as discussed previously [4]. They allow an efficient creation of knowledge maps and the Internet enables updates, independent from specific locations. The maintenance of extensive knowledge assets can be very important while managing emergent processes. To use that knowledge efficiently, it must be structured accordingly. Both can be achieved through BPM design systems.

Emergent business processes are also an interesting application area for reference models. Reference models provide knowledge about business processes (or information systems in general) in a structured, easy-to-apply format [5].

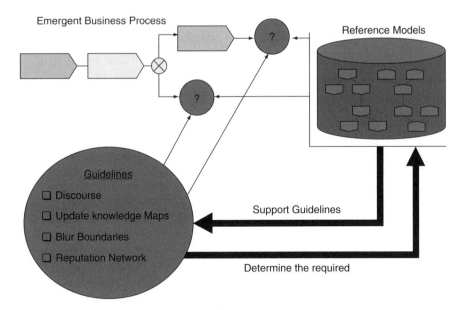

Fig. 8.4 Using reference models to support the management of emergent processes

They can be used as the basis for evaluating and defining the next steps of emergent processes, based on the current execution results. They can facilitate the discourse required for the management of emergence. The use of such knowledge components leads to significant advantages because it hastens the discourse and ensures usable results.

The use of reference models to support the management of emergent processes in MPE is visualized in Fig. 8.4.

The use of reference models not only supports the necessary discourse. On the one hand, the models can be the basis for developing knowledge maps, support the communication and interaction with people outside the organization, and help recognize and verify a special reputation and know-how. On the other hand, the guidelines for managing emergence and the scope of the emergent process also help to select appropriate reference models that can be applied in a specific initiative.

Although management behavior is most important for a successful approach toward emergent processes, the discussed infrastructure delivers key support. It makes the management behavior more efficient and bridges great distances, necessary for work in an international environment.

8.4 The Bottom Line

Emergent business processes are knowledge-intensive processes in which the outcomes are unpredictable (Sect. 8.1).

Participants in emergent processes must continuously make sense of their situation and decide, in real time, on the next steps to take (Sect. 8.1).

- Managers contribute to high performance when they are able to manage their employees to effectively handle unpredictability in the workplace and market-place – and by doing so, turn routine business and processes into emergent ones (Sect. 8.1).
- An infrastructure supporting emergence is clearly critical. Just as critical is what managers should do while workers are carrying out their emergent processes (Sect. 8.1).
- The work process in which managers of emergent processes engage is what we call streaming together "participatory innovative spurts" (Sect. 8.1).
- Four key management activities (guidelines) are necessary to manage emergent processes: continuously engage in discourse with participants; dynamically update knowledge maps to continuously rematch participant responsibilities; purposely blur boundaries between who is inside and outside the organization; govern through egocentric reputation networks, not rules (Sect. 8.2).
- The activities of managing emergent processes require changes and extensions in traditional managerial work (Sect. 8.2).
- The concept of Enterprise 2.0+ helps to implement and enable the application of those guidelines to manage emergent processes (Sect. 8.3).
- BPM modeling systems can also be used to make the management of emergent processes more efficient (Sect. 8.3).
- Emergent business processes comprise an interesting application area for reference models (Sect. 8.3).

References

1. Davenport, T: Thinking for a Living – How to Get Better Performance and Results from Knowledge Workers. Harvard Business School Press, Boston (2005)
2. Majchrzak, A, Logan, D, McCurdy, R, Kirchmer, M: Four keys to managing emergence. MIT Sloan Manag. Review **47**, 14–18 (2006)
3. Majchrzak, A, Logan, D, McCurdy, R, Kirchmer, M: What business leaders can learn from Jazz musicians about emergent processes. In: Scheer, A-W, Kruppke, H, Jost, W, Kindermann, H (eds.) Agility by ARIS Business Process Management. Springer, Berlin/New York/Others (2006)
4. IDS Scheer AG. (ed.): ARIS Platform. Product Brochure. IDS Scheer, Saarbruecken (2007)
5. Fettke, P, Loos, P: Perspectives on reference modeling. In: Fettke, P, Loos, P (eds.) Reference Modeling for Business Systems Analysis, pp. 1–20. Idea group publishing, Hershey/London (2007)

Chapter 9
Globalization Requires MPE

Globalization is a megatrend that influences the business environment tremendously. Although the world was once dominated by the economies of Europe, North America, and Japan, there are now new players emerging: China, India, Russia, and Brazil, among others. There is no doubt that globalization is changing the world in which we do business. Most successful enterprises work with customers, suppliers, and other market partners in multiple countries around the world. They often have subsidiaries with operations in various countries on different continents. As Friedman says, "the world has become flat" [1]. For example, a midsized manufacturer of highly sophisticated machinery tools focused on the Canadian and US markets. Step by step, the company began to follow its customers and prospects (various manufacturing companies) to Europe, opened a plant in Germany, then onto Brazil and China. Thus, the company became a player in the global market. The financial markets are linked through high-speed networks so transactions can be executed all over the world, essentially in real time.

There are many factors that bring the world closer together, such as [1]:

- The fall of the Berlin Wall and the resulting opening of Eastern Europe.
- The rise of the World Wide Web.
- New Web-based workflow software, based on standards, connecting the world.
- Powerful communities, like Open Source initiatives, to develop software.
- Outsourcing, or the execution of processes or subprocesses of an enterprise by service providers (e.g., located in India).
- Offshoring, or the transition of entire enterprise units (e.g., a production unit) into another country, such as China.
- Supply chain processes as a source of competitive advantage.
- Insourcing (e.g., UPS moved from a "package delivery company" to a global logistics service provider, conveniently offering all necessary logistics services through its own resources).
- Informing, referring to search engines like Google, which provide any sort of required information in seconds.

M. Kirchmer, *High Performance Through Process Excellence*,
DOI 10.1007/978-3-642-21165-2_9, © Springer-Verlag Berlin Heidelberg 2011

• Digitalization, mobility, personalization, and virtualization.

All of these factors encourage, or even force, enterprises to work across the boundaries of continents and countries as they strive for high performance. Consequently, they must develop business processes in a global business environment. On a strategic level, Bartlett and Ghoshal distinguish four types of companies working across country borders [2]:

• Multinational companies
• International companies
• Global companies
• Transnational companies

In multinational companies, the subsidiaries are more or less independent units that are only required by headquarters to have a certain financial performance. Subsidiaries are typically run as self-sufficient enterprises. In international companies, the transfer of knowledge from headquarters to the subsidiaries is more important; the controls are better developed. Global organizations are even more centralized; the subsidiaries are tightly controlled. In a centralized organizational structure, the world is seen as a single economic entity. Transnational companies consist of networks of interdependent specialized units in various countries. Subsidiaries have different roles. Knowledge is developed jointly and shared internationally.

Although the transnational enterprise seems to be the most efficient and effective, the other forms of internationalization are also valid in specific phases of the life cycle of an organization, depending on company-specific strategies [3]. A startup company that wants to quickly enter international markets may choose to do so as a multinational or international organization and then gradually become a global and then a transnational enterprise. At IDS Scheer, I was part of a team transforming a national company into a multinational enterprise with subsidiaries around the world and eventually into a global company. Accenture, where I have been working since 2008, is clearly a transnational company, with knowledge centers around the world.

All of those enterprise structures require the appropriate business processes to be implemented successfully across locations in the different countries. The management of process excellence (MPE) approach described previously can be used to manage those processes. But what are specific influence factors of the global business environment? Do they result in any particular MPE tasks or a special infrastructure? These questions are discussed in this chapter, which focuses on the design and implementation phase of MPE, as visualized in Fig. 9.1.

Although every phase of process management is naturally impacted by the international environment, key measures for overcoming resulting challenges through globalization are taken during design and implementation. The resulting business processes can be executed and controlled using the presented MPE approach in all local company subsidiaries.

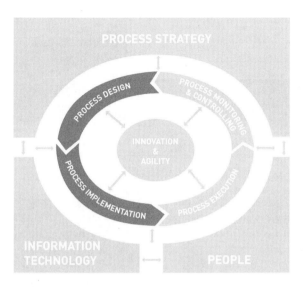

Fig. 9.1 Focus on design and implementation phase of MPE

9.1 Some Personal Impressions

During my time at IDS Scheer, I was able to gain quite a bit of international management experience. IDS Scheer is a German software and consulting company with subsidiaries in more than 20 countries around the world. While working for more than 6 years in Europe, mostly in Germany but also in France and other countries, I managed consulting units. After that, I lived in the United States for more than 10 years, holding several different management responsibilities, mostly general management as head of the region. In between, I worked for a year in Japan and assumed responsibility for overall business in the country for 5 years. Now, working for Accenture, I am continuing an international focus and can even gather additional experiences, e.g. while working with my colleagues in India.

I found the differences between working in the United States and Japan extremely interesting and learned a lot "on the job." I would like to discuss some of those experiences because I believe they can help others learn what it means to manage business processes in an international environment. Because I was born and raised in Germany, I share my observations from a German perspective.

Most US offices in typical companies are composed of cubicles, as shown in Fig. 9.2. The cubicles offer employees a certain degree of privacy – everyone has her or his own little kingdom. In most cases, executives have offices, of which location and size show the importance of the position, as indicated on top of Fig. 9.2.

A Japanese office looks very different, as you can see in Fig. 9.3. People sit in rows, one person next to another. People are courteous, so not to disturb one another. Employees feel like they are part of a "family." Even executives are typically integrated in that environment. Their desks are in the same room, just positioned separately to oversee their employees.

Fig. 9.2   Office in the United States

Fig. 9.3   Office in Japan

This first impression I share indicates some major differences regarding the behavior of employees in the work environment, which we will briefly discuss. In the United States, everyone behaves as an entrepreneur, primarily focusing on their own interests and goals. Employees are moved into the company direction through appropriately structured compensation and formal measures, such as job descriptions, policies, and procedures. Company policies play an important role, ensuring employee rights, but also protecting the employer company on a legal level. People in the United States are often accustomed or at least open to multicultural work environments. Companies can assemble teams with members from multiple countries and enable them to move the company forward, using the strengths of each individual. However, in most states, employment is "at will." In other words, people can leave on any given day – a situation that is legally impossible in many European countries (e.g., in Germany where employees have to give notice well in advance). Therefore, employers must manage people accordingly, on the one hand motivating them to encourage them to stay with the company, and on the other hand, always preparing for a situation where a key employee leaves. People in a US work environment seem to be very open and direct; however, you often have to read between the lines to understand what they really mean. If someone calls a presentation "great," it does not necessarily mean that he really liked a presentation. A follow-up invitation says much more. People are generally self-confident and convinced of the superior quality of their capabilities. A "we are the best" mentality is common. Therefore, it is often not easy for a foreigner to criticize someone in a way that would not upset him. One must criticize positively, so people learn quickly and support necessary actions.

In a Japanese work environment, the situation is quite different. People smile often and are friendlier than those in a US environment. This goes so far that it is generally considered impolite to answer a question with "no." But "yes" does not always mean "yes." I remember when I asked a Japanese colleague if he had sent out a specific letter and he answered "yes – but not yet." At the time I was very surprised, but now I understand that he just wanted to be polite. Conflicts that would require a "no" are often carried out "undercover," (e.g., through e-mails). In Japan, people typically pay close attention to detail. You may receive a schedule with an elaborate color code – but this also takes time. Do not expect a high-speed environment. However, people finish what they start, so you can expect results. People in Japan are accustomed to very long working hours. Some of my colleagues started the day between 9 and 10 a.m., but they rarely went home before 11 p.m. or midnight. And their commute involved a 1–2 h train ride. In general, I found it difficult to encourage creativity and the development of new ideas. In most cases, some external input is required. Once you have hired an employee in Japan, you can depend on loyalty. People do not leave their jobs easily.

Although globalization brings the behaviors of employees closer together, it is still important to know about country-specific behaviors when designing and implementing business processes. This is especially the case for manually executed processes and subprocesses or necessary teamwork activities.

Country-specific differences are not only observed within the office, but also in customer-facing behavior and the habits around business transactions. In the United

States, there is generally a very high customer focus. The customer is just as important as the product. The quality and performance of a product are demonstrated through the customers using that product. This is a big difference from many German enterprises, where people love their products and think in terms of functions and features. In the United States, the characteristic of "invented here" is very important. The aforementioned self-confidence and pride often makes it difficult for foreign companies with foreign products to enter the market. In general, the created perception of a company and its offerings is very important. Perception is often considered reality; therefore, marketing is extremely important in the promotion of products. For the IT market, industry analysts, including The Gartner Group, Forrester, AMR or IDC, play an important role. In many cases, customers rely on analyst research to support their buying decisions. Change and speed are very common in the United States. Executives switch companies, sometimes even on a quarterly basis, projects start and stop quickly, contact persons change. Change is the only stable part of business, which often leads to short-term viewpoints. In many cases, it is difficult to sell solutions with long-term impacts. "Why should I care what happens next quarter or even next year?" is a common attitude.

The attitude is very different in Japan and continuity is important to many people. Although globalization has already changed many things, people still try to reduce the speed of change and keep a well-controlled pace. They are very careful. You will often have the same contact person at a client over many years. Executives stick with their companies and you can count on their commitments. The characteristic of "invented here" is not nearly as important as it is in the United States. On the contrary, American and European products are well accepted. Trust is the key in business life. It counts more than contracts, which can cause conflicts with Western accounting requirements for formal paperwork. Business decisions are often heavily influenced by personal relations and less by general perception. Business meals are very important in Japan. True negotiations often occur during dinner, in a very casual atmosphere. The formal negotiations are simply a means to revisit the arguments and conclusions discussed previously.

These customer- and market-related behaviors are again important for the design and implementation of business processes. It is essential to be aware of those particularities when a company standard business process is defined and rolled out in a specific country.

The following are some general lessons I learned while working and living in Germany, France, the United States, and Japan. They can be applied in the management of processes in an international environment or work in different countries:

- Listen, listen, and listen: Do not think you already know everything. Hear what the local employees have to say.
- Even in a very unfamiliar environment, always look on the bright side of things: This keeps you in a good mood with a positive attitude.
- Accept differences wherever possible: Different countries have different habits – in most cases, it is best to accept that as fact.
- Communicate clearly what you do not accept: When you intentionally do not want to support certain habits, it is important for the people around you to know that.

- Show that you are interested in being integrated: Generally, local people are proud to make you part of their community, but you have to show that you are willing to accept and support that integration.
- Clarify and explain the value you bring to the table: People have to know why you are in another country and what the benefits are to them personally.
- Share your interests and introduce yourself as a "private person," not just a "business person": People work with and accept people, not just positions or roles.

These were some of my personal impressions about global business and what it means for managers and the processes for which they are responsible. So, what are the key influence factors of globalization on business processes and how do they impact processes? How does globalization change processes?

9.2 Globalization Changes Processes

Globalization leads to processes carried out in several countries or influences business processes in one or more countries. Therefore, country-specific factors influence those processes. Examples of such influence factors include the following:

- Legal system
- Geography
- Culture
- Education
- Language

The legal system provides country-specific regulations that that must be reflected in processes. For example, tax regulations influence finance processes, but can also lead to modifications in the supply chain. Human resources (HR) administrative processes (e.g., in the payroll area) are another example of processes often influenced by legal regulations. The geography of a country can also influence processes, such as the transportation planning and management of goods in transit. Specific cultural aspects also influence processes. The focus on details in Japan may necessitate a modified process design in comparison with the design in Western countries, where too much detail may be perceived as having a negative impact on the personal work environment. A country's average level of education can influence process design and implementation. Highly automated processes in countries with little expertise may not make sense. Even the languages spoken in different countries can influence processes: you may not be able to use certain software systems for the process execution because they do not support specific languages (e.g., Asian languages). Specific local vendor expertise can determine other influence factors (e.g., for local application systems). These influence factors are shown in Fig. 9.4.

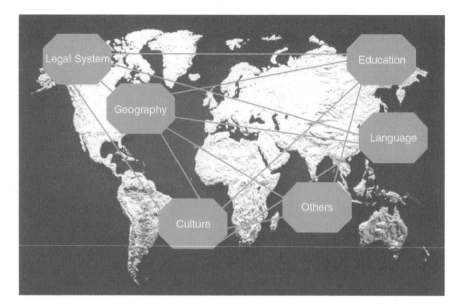

Fig. 9.4 Country-specific influence factors on processes

Such influence factors impact business processes and typically lead to country-specific variants of processes that can be carried out in subsidiaries or in a central headquarters location.

Such factors also influence the business process management (BPM) approach in and of itself, the "process of process management." MPE must address the impacts of the global business environment, and in turn manage the influence of the presented factors. This situation is visualized in Fig. 9.5.

The factors can either influence the business processes directly or indirectly through product variants. Country-specific requirements may lead to modified products that necessitate additional engineering activities, leading to new production and logistics requirements. This results in new or modified processes in various areas of an organization. The direct and indirect influences of country-specific factors are demonstrated in Fig. 9.6.

We have previously discussed one example of country-specific processes. In a Japanese environment, the focus on quality can lead to planned redundancies of quality control activities. This may not be acceptable in Western organizations focused on cost and time efficiency. As mentioned, country-specific tax regulations can impact logistics processes. For example, in the United States, you can select storage locations for specific goods on the basis of state tax regulations. In France, where taxes are the same across the entire country, this selection criterion does not need to be applied. The related logistics process is simplified, as visualized in Fig. 9.7.

In a vast country like the United States, it has become increasingly difficult to conduct face-to-face meetings – especially due to increasing cost and time

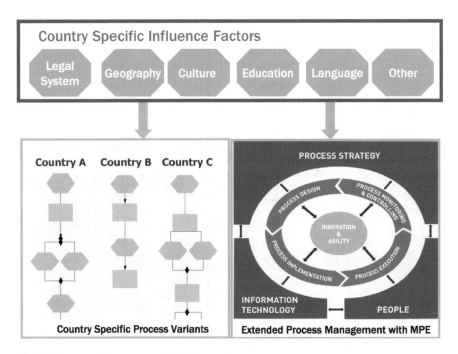

Fig. 9.5 Impacts of country-specific influence factors

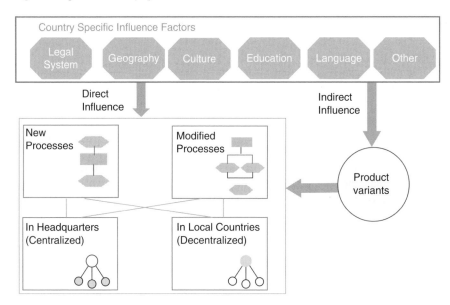

Fig. 9.6 Direct and indirect influence of country-specific factors on processes

requirements. Therefore, the use of Web-based remote presentations and meetings is extremely important and part of many sales processes. In a geographically smaller country, such as Germany, this may not be as important. Most of the cities

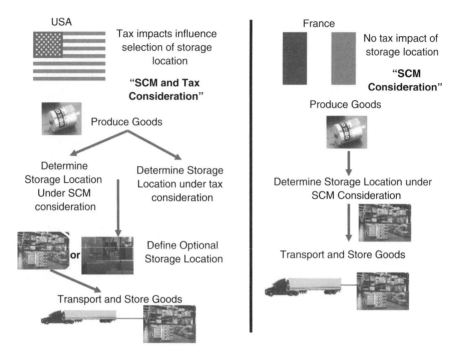

Fig. 9.7 Example: legal regulations influence processes

are close enough to be reached by car or train. This influence of country-specific factors on processes is shown in Fig. 9.8.

Even the language of a country can influence processes. For example, Japanese or Chinese language characters require specific printing capabilities. But there may be a requirement for certain documents, such as invoices, to be printed in a language that can be checked by centralized global departments. Therefore, the same document may need to be printed a second time in a Western language, resulting in process variants, as shown in Fig. 9.9.

There are many other country-specific influence factors. Therefore, a company should evaluate the specific influence factors of countries where it has subsidiaries or market partners involved in a business process. An example is the difference in the voltage between US and European countries. A company producing electric motors in the United States must develop country variants of its products to deliver its offerings to Europe. These product variants can lead to new or additional activities in the entire organization, and ultimately to modified processes. Additional product variants must be designed, handled throughout the logistics processes, and reflected in marketing and sales processes. This situation is explained in Fig. 9.10.

The global business environment directly or indirectly influences the design of business processes and their implementation. In general, customer-facing processes, subprocesses, and offerings must be localized. Support processes or

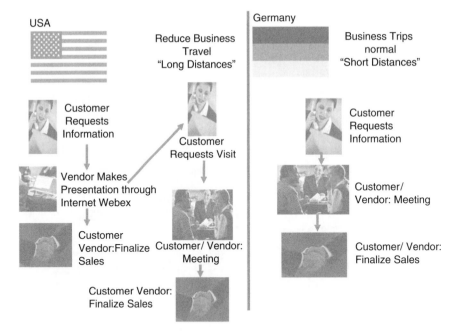

Fig. 9.8 Example: geography influences processes

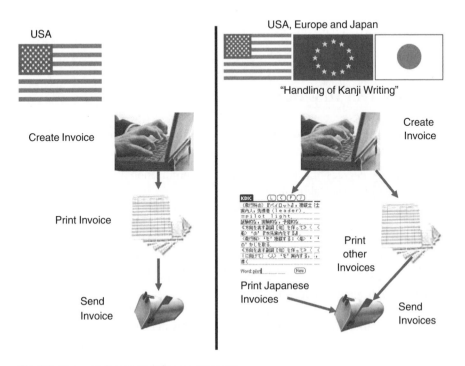

Fig. 9.9 Example: languages influence processes

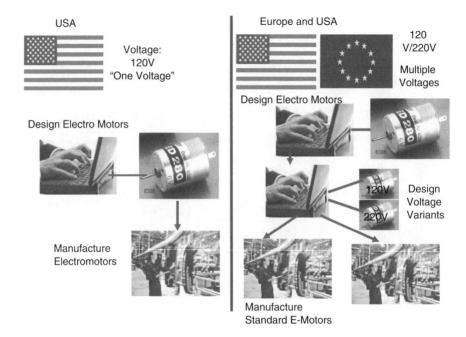

Fig. 9.10 Example: other country-specific factors influence processes

back-office activities can typically be standardized. The influence of globalization must be reflected in the MPE approach.

9.3 How Can MPE Help?

On the basis of the discussion thus far, we can identify necessary steps to handle global business environments within MPE:

- Identify the degrees of centralization and decentralization of business processes according to globalization strategy.
- Define country-specific influence factors, especially for customer-facing processes and offerings.
- Identify the impact of those factors on the design and implementation of business processes (and the other MPE phases, if applicable).
- Modify the process design according to the country impacts.

The centralization and decentralization of processes reflects the general strategy, leading to international, multinational, global, or transnational organizations, as explained. In this instance, the positioning of the innovation process is very important in a MPE approach. To benefit from the international input, this process must be integrated in corporate and subsidiary activities (e.g., to support the idea finding). The integration of international third parties, such as customers, universities, or research institutions, can also support the global environment.

Country-specific influence factors can be defined on the basis of the reference list discussed previously. Additional factors must be added and those that are not relevant should be deleted. Then, the business impact of those country-specifics is defined, as presented in the aforementioned examples. The closer the processes are to the local customers, the stronger the localization requirements. The country-specific factors lead to great impacts. In addition, processes related to the design and production of offerings must deal with these localization requirements. General activities and support processes can often be centralized, or at least standardized, across countries. The influence of country-specific factors is smaller. The business impact of country-specific influence factors are incorporated in the design of the business processes in the MPE process factory.

In process design within a globally active organization, one "master process" can be used to develop one or several process variants for decentralized country-specific processes. Therefore, one must manage process variants over the entire business process life cycle and continuously update the design. Changes in the business environment can relate to one or several of the process variants. They may be triggered globally through a change in the master process or locally through changes in the country-specific business environment. This activity must be organized through the process governance and is generally supported by the previously discussed BPM software systems [4]. The management of process variants is visualized in Fig. 9.11.

The discussed reference models can deliver initial solutions to those processes. They must now be modified according to the country requirements. With the increasing importance of global business aspects for nearly every organization, the development of reference models with country-specific content will also become highly relevant. Content providers may progressively move toward this direction and offer reference models related to such topics of globalization.

The utilization of standard application software systems or software components developed for global use simplifies the implementation of processes in a globally acting organization. Standard software typically supports the following aspects, which are important for the realization of country-specific processes:

- Multiple currencies
- Multiple languages
- Multiple units of measurement
- Various legal standards
- International documentation
- International rollout strategies
- International hotline/support
- Others

This is visualized in Fig. 9.12.

Change management activities must be adapted to the countries involved in the implementation of a business process. This may include multiple ways of

Master Model ┊ Country specific Process Variants

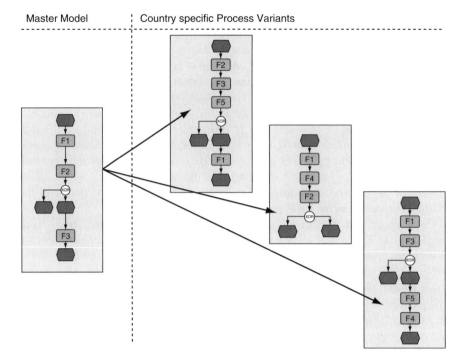

Fig. 9.11 Management of process variants

representing process models. Information, communication, and training must also be adapted to the country-specific habits.

The advantages of BPM software systems can be especially well applied in global business environments because the data volume to be handled increases and the remote work with process models becomes more and more important. The probability of changes in the business environment also increases, resulting in higher maintenance frequencies for the business process models in the process warehouse. MPE delivers the appropriate infrastructure to handle those challenges of a global BPM environment and enable high performance across the global enterprise.

9.4   The Bottom Line

- It is especially important to know about country-specific influences in the cases of manually executed processes and subprocesses or necessary teamwork activities (Sect. 9.1).
- Country-specific behaviors of employees and customers are important for the design and implementation of business processes (Sect. 9.1).
- Specific lessons learned can support the management of processes in a global environment (Sect. 9.1).

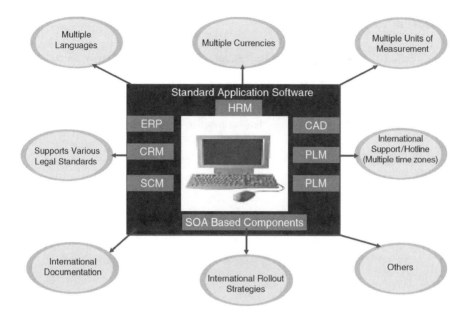

Fig. 9.12 Standard software supports globalization

- Globalization leads to processes carried out in several countries or influencing business processes in one or more countries. Therefore, country-specific factors influence those processes (Sect. 9.2).
- Those country-specific influence factors impact business processes, especially customer-facing processes and processes related to the design and production of offerings. In most cases, this impact leads to country-specific variants of processes (Sect. 9.2).
- The country-specific influence factors also influence the business process management (BPM) approach itself, the "process of process management." MPE must reflect that (Sect. 9.2).
- The country-specific factors can either influence the business processes directly or indirectly through product (offering) variants (Sect. 9.2).
- MPE includes the necessary steps to handle global business environments (Sect. 9.3).
- In the design processes of a global environment, one "master processes" is often used to develop one or several process variants for decentralized country-specific processes (Sect. 9.3).
- The utilization of standard application software systems developed for global use simplifies the implementation of processes in a globally acting organization (Sect. 9.3).
- MPE delivers the appropriate infrastructure to handle the challenges of a global BPM environment (Sect. 9.3).

References

1. Friedman, T L: The World Is Flat – A Brief History of the Twenty-First Century. Farrar, Straus and Giroux, New York (2005)
2. Bartlett, C A, Ghoshal, S: Managing Across Borders – The Transnational Solution. Harvard Business School Press, Boston (2002)
3. Scheer, A-W: Start-ups are Easy, But. ... Springer, Berlin/New York (2001)
4. IDS Scheer AG. (ed.): ARIS Platform. Product Brochure. IDS Scheer, Saarbruecken (2007)

Chapter 10
Small and Medium Enterprises Also Benefit from MPE

Small and medium enterprises (SMEs) are playing an increasingly important role in the global business environment. New companies are founded as startups or spin-offs of larger organizations. Others disappear for various reasons. But the overall number *keeps* growing. For example, more than 90% of all firms in the European Union are considered as SMEs [1]. Also, larger companies often organize their divisions as small enterprises that conduct business like other mid-market firms.

SMEs have to be faster and more agile than large organizations if they are to achieve high performance. Because they do not have any significant economy of scale, speed and agility is the only way to survive. They must also be very focused on innovation to justify their existence. While large organizations can quickly follow trends in the business environment and leverage their size to be successful, SMEs do not have that lever. They are generally built on innovative business ideas that make them unique. More and more often, business process innovation plays the key role, as we have discussed previously.

An increasing number of software and consulting companies focus a segment of their offerings on SME. The mid-market is not only considered to be dynamic, but also has a growing demand for enterprise-wide solutions. SMEs have become interesting customers for many suppliers in the IT market.

While working at IDS Scheer, I worked with some colleagues to launch several mid-market initiatives to bring elements of business process management (BPM) to those organizations. In addition, I managed IDS Scheer subsidiaries in the Americas and Asia for more than 10 years – subsidiaries that were similar to typical SMEs. At Accenture, I am part of the team that is building a business unit around process excellence topics, just as one might build an SME. This chapter is based on a combination of experiences in both fields: working at a service and software provider for SMEs and managing such an organization myself.

In this chapter, the definition of SME is discussed briefly and some key characteristics of mid-market organizations are presented. Why are SMEs special? Are their BPM requirements really different than large organizations? What does that mean for Management of Process Excellence? Do SMEs need MPE too?

M. Kirchmer, *High Performance Through Process Excellence*,
DOI 10.1007/978-3-642-21165-2_10, © Springer-Verlag Berlin Heidelberg 2011

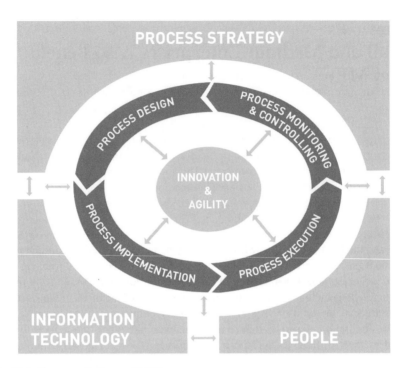

Fig. 10.1 Focus on all phases of MPE

As we discuss these topics, they are relevant for all phases of the MPE approach, as shown in Fig. 10.1.

10.1 Definition and Characteristics of SMEs

If you look through literature for a clear and globally valid definition of SMEs, you will not find one. Also, the criteria to define this market used by vendors to mid-market businesses are not consistent, often showing significant differences. However, there are certain commonalities. In most publications, enterprises are defined as SMEs, based on two major criteria:

- Revenue
- Number of employees

One or both of these criteria must fall under a certain limit. However, the limits are generally defined differently in different countries or by different organizations. For example, a company with less than 500 people is considered an SME in Germany; but that limit could be 100 employees in Belgium [1]. Companies considered SMEs in the United States may already be viewed as large businesses in some European countries. These country-specific definitions demonstrate that there is currently no definition of SME that is generally accepted on a global level. In many situations, this is not necessary because many SMEs have a strong regional focus, but more and more companies considered to be SMEs are also working internationally. Successful SMEs participate in globalization. They are often part of international inter-enterprise processes. Therefore, for the purposes of this book, we will introduce a general definition for SME that I believe can be applied across country boundaries.

As mentioned previously, many large companies are organized as networks, in which every unit represents a small- or medium-sized business. Such companies are often working in a global environment. The topics discussed in this chapter are relevant for business units of these large companies, too.

In the United States, solution vendors often consider organizations with revenue up to $1 billion das medium companies. This is most likely the broadest SME definition, including all companies that could be somehow considered SMEs. However, this broad definition produces a very heterogeneous group of companies that is difficult to characterize. In most cases, a company with $1 billion in revenue will have very different requirements and characteristics than a company with $10 million in revenue. Such a broad definition does not enable the definition of a targeted BPM approach.

In general, the characteristics discussed in this chapter best apply to companies with $50–500 million in revenue and approximately 100–500 employees. This definition includes organizations with one or several locations in one or multiple countries. A small or medium enterprise can be an independent organization or a subsidiary of a larger company that is essentially operated as a self-sufficient unit. This is the type of companies we will discuss in this chapter about SMEs.

Most mid-market organizations have characteristics that challenge the implementation of BPM solutions, especially the execution of business processes, based on enterprise resource planning (ERP) systems and the previously other discussed IT-based execution solutions, like service-oriented architectures (SOA). However, SMEs also have attributes that simplify the rollout of business process-oriented approaches. We will now discuss both types of characteristics.

In looking at the group of characteristics that create challenges in applying a BPM approach to achieve high performance, the following SME attributes stand out [2]:

- Cost pressure
- Time pressure
- Human resource capacity
- Multiple roles of employees
- Skill level
- Others

SMEs are often under tremendous cost pressure. They may be funded through venture capital or smaller, private budgets. In many cases, the owner of the company has invested his or her own money in the company. Therefore, the cost of BPM solutions plays a key role. Often, SMEs simply cannot afford infrastructure investments even if they feel the benefits. Other times, they just do not want to take the risk of bringing in additional money or new investors.

The low number of employees in smaller organizations precludes them from staffing projects over a long time period, resulting in a great time pressure for any initiative. There is no budget to increase the number of people, the resource capacity. People must focus on vital, day-to-day operations. Time for BPM initiatives, which have to be started as projects, is very limited. Project team members are normally only available on a part-time basis. Even small changes in the business environment can have major resource impacts relative to the overall company size.

Once processes must be executed, the personnel restrictions again come into play. Employees often play multiple roles. BPM approaches need to blend into that environment. There is little or no time for additional tasks. In many cases, hiring new employees is impossible, due to the previously discussed budget restrictions. BPM has to be implemented in a manner that is well integrated with the other multiple tasks of SME employees.

Mid-market organizations generally have no well-developed IT or organizational departments. They often consider those fields to be pure overhead that must be kept to a minimum level. Therefore, SMEs are lacking sufficient IT skills and method or tool know-how necessary to take care of a BPM infrastructure. The development of the talent needed to start and manage the organization based on the principles of BPM is a key challenge.

However, SMEs also have characteristics that simplify the rollout of BPM approaches – characteristics that contribute to the success of BPM and truly support the company goals to achieve high performance [2]:

- Fast decision making
- Integration of activities
- Employee work ethic
- Others

Most mid-market organizations can ensure fast decisions. In many cases, the company owner himself or herself decides, without many meetings or discussions. Even if there is a more collaborative decision-making process in place, the number of involved people is considerably lower than in large organizations. The result is increased speed in start up of initiatives once they are accepted by top management. Even the fact that human resources are in short supply has positive side effects: SMEs are truly forced to focus on the important key aspects of BPM and make them happen quickly and efficiently – all of which is driven effectively by top management.

The small size of the organizations leads to a "natural" integration of business activities. People are accustomed to working in a business process-oriented manner and understand how things fit together. This is the positive side of people playing multiple roles. In many cases, this integration even crosses company boundaries. SMEs know their customers and suppliers, as well as their other market partners. Sometimes, a few very dominating clients will deliver input about the organization of inter-enterprise processes. Intra- and inter-enterprise business processes are not distributed over many organizational units in SMEs because their organizational structure is generally much simpler than that of a large organization, which has to build more complex structures to get their many employees focused on specific tasks. For large organizations to leverage size, their employees are often specialized on single tasks, ultimately challenging their integration and management in one business process. SME employees performing multiple tasks of a process can be more easily organized into a process-based structure.

In many cases, SME employees have a proactive and result-oriented work attitude. They are accustomed to recognizing, analyzing, and resolving upcoming challenges. They do not have many guidelines and policies on which to rely. People must act – quickly and efficiently – in order to be successful. The company depends on them figuring out the best possible actions. This simplifies the implementation of a BPM approach and the related activities. The governance model can be less complicated and rely on the employees' solutions-oriented working style.

The key characteristics of SMEs are shown in Fig. 10.2. Although this list is surely not complete, it highlights the most important aspects to be considered. These characteristics set the guidelines for an efficient and effective approach to BPM in SME.

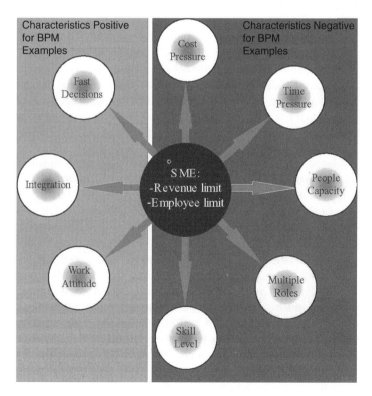

Fig. 10.2 Characteristics of small and medium enterprises

What does that mean for the rollout of a BPM approach in an SME? How can an organization meet the presented challenges and utilize the SME-specific strengths? What does it mean to manage business processes in an SME environment to enable high performance and move quickly from strategy to operations?

10.2   How Do Those Characteristics Impact Business Process Management?

The discussed characteristics have direct impacts on a BPM approach applied in SMEs. They deliver the requirements necessary for an SME to really benefit from a business process-oriented organization.

Because of the cost pressure in an SME environment, BPM must be delivered in a very efficient manner. The request for fixed-price proposals to deliver BPM services and products is common. SMEs have to focus on core activities of BPM, delivering the results that are most important. Applying the BPM approach around the entire process life cycle may restrict the development of an infrastructure, based on the most important key aspects of this life cycle, which must be identified at the beginning of a BPM initiative. Some of those key elements can be predefined, but others have to be added later, depending on the specific enterprise. Nice-to-have features are generally not affordable; a minimalist approach to BPM is desired. This can often be best achieved by defining BPM solutions packages, covering the entire life cycle, including design, implementation, execution, and process controlling.

As a consequence of the time constraints, BPM approaches must be implemented in short projects of weeks or a few months, not several months or years. This goes hand in hand with the described definition of a clear BPM focus. Successful BPM within SMEs requires easy-to-use methods and tools to keep change management activities to a minimum, ultimately saving cost and time while enabling the efficient use of existing SME resources. During process execution and controlling, related BPM activities should be integrated seamlessly into the day-to-day work, ensuring again the highest efficiency.

Because employees play multiple roles, they require a process execution that allows for the combination of many different tasks. Appropriate "process components" must be defined so they can be handled by one person. The BPM infrastructure has to support this structure, especially during execution and controlling of business processes, so that high performance can be achieved with the same or very similar number of employees. Traditional, function-oriented activities must be replaced through process-oriented work steps; a transition period is generally impossible.

Because of the skill level in SMEs, BPM solutions must be implemented and later maintained with a relatively low level of specialized BPM and IT skills. Again, easy-to-use and straightforward approaches to implementing solutions are preferred to very sophisticated approaches. SMEs cannot typically afford to increase their skill levels in those areas to the level to which large organizations are accustomed. Once again, integrated BPM solution packages can alleviate this situation.

Outsourcing some of the infrastructure can be another helpful solution. New concepts, like procuring "software-as-a service," are often very attractive to SMEs because they are able to avoid the necessity to build highly specialized skills, while reducing the necessary budgets and capital.

Fast decisions enable handling the time constraints in BPM implementations. They also reduce cost for lengthy analyses and studies often required by larger organizations to prepare for a more sophisticated and complex decision-making process. They support the necessary flexibility during the execution and controlling activities. Fast decisions can become a key enabler for the agility that BPM can deliver. They drive strategies quickly into operations. The BPM governance to be established must ensure that this SME advantage is applied effectively.

Because people know how things fit together due to their multiple roles and the natural integration in SME, they can easily understand and appreciate the process thinking necessary to ensure the best results for the final customer of an end-to-end business process. This people skill must be utilized systematically and simplifies the analysis of the existing business situation, as well as the design and implementation phase. In addition, it reduces the change management needs, especially in regard to training. The tight collaboration with customers and suppliers enables the inclusion of inter-enterprise processes in the early phases of a BPM initiative. This is often crucial for SMEs because they have to focus on their specific role in a business network. The active use of the natural integration in SMEs is a key success factor in BPM initiatives. Again, this must be reflected in an appropriate governance approach.

The positive work attitude simplifies the implementation of BPM as a new approach to managing an organization. Successful BPM initiatives in SMEs must take advantage of the fact that employees are accustomed to dealing with new situations and change. They are open to BPM and support the rollout. An active knowledge transfer in the early phases of BPM will ensure that employees can quickly become drivers of the BPM efforts. This is another aspect for an appropriate process governance approach.

BPM solution and software vendors reflect SME-specific requirements in solution packages. One example includes IDS Scheer's industry-specific ARIS SmartPath solutions [2]. We will discuss this solution more in detail to understand the possibility of BPM-related offerings targeted to midsize companies. This is an example of the application of the discussed requirements and is presented here because it fits well with the aspects of BPM discussed in this book. Other examples include Accenture's solutions for SME (e.g., in the resource-related industries, especially chemicals).

The ARIS SmartPath overall architecture is based on ARIS, the previously described process architecture for the efficient and effective design of business processes [3, 4]. The solution leads organizations on a "smart path" to master future business challenges. It helps to design, implement, execute, and control processes in an efficient and effective manner. During the implementation, a "smart path" for rapid and cost-efficient project success is chosen. This means the solution covers all aspects of BPM and delivers input for an appropriate governance model.

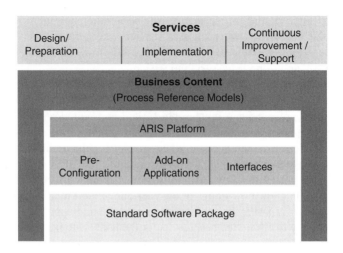

Fig. 10.3 ARIS SmartPath – solution architecture

ARIS SmartPath consists of three major components:

- Application software, such as ERP
- Customer relationship management (CRM) and Supply chain management (SCM) systems (based on SAP)
- Business content in form of reference models in the ARIS Platform
- Consulting services

These components are consolidated into one solutions package that can be offered at a fixed price and delivered in an efficient and effective way to meet SME cost and time requirements. It also includes an early knowledge transfer and the definition of an appropriate process governance approach. The solution architecture of ARIS SmartPath [2] is shown in Fig. 10.3.

At the core of the solution is a standard application software product, which is enhanced by an industry-specific preconfiguration and add-on software components, as well as standard interfaces. This application software is combined with the design and performance management component of the ARIS Platform [5], which we discussed earlier. The ARIS Platform contains the necessary business content in the form of business process reference models. On the basis of this content, the pre-implementation, implementation, and post-implementation services are provided in a process-oriented approach. The standard application software ensures the future execution of the processes.

The application software can be preconfigured to support the processes (e.g., of a specific industry). Add-on applications and interfaces for the applicable standard application software are developed in customer-specific projects or purchased from third-party software vendors. This enables support of additional business scenarios (e.g., inter-enterprise business processes). The industry-specific pre-configurations are generally more detailed than standard industry solutions delivered by broad software vendors [6]. These pre-configured software solutions are another way to save time and increase resource efficiency during the implementation. Business content is delivered in the form of business process reference models. These reference models support effective process design, based on best practices. Services are offered for general project work, the definition of the required process governance model, as well as hotline and helpdesk support during process execution and controlling. These services ensure the smooth transition from design to execution and support continuous improvement.

This SME solution example can now be generalized. It delivers input for the use of MPE in an SME environment. We now know the SME requirements for BPM approaches and we have seen an example of how those requirements can be addressed. What does that mean for MPE? Where does the broader MPE approach deliver additional value?

10.3   What Does It All Mean for MPE?

The key deliverables of MPE – innovation and agility, based on smart decisions and fast execution – fit well with the overall characteristics of SMEs. Therefore, the philosophy of MPE supports the key challenges of SMEs to be fast and innovative to survive and achieve high performance. MPE is well positioned to truly enable SMEs to become high-performance businesses.

The fast decisions and the natural integration of activities within SME also fit well with the MPE philosophy. MPE enables the development of SME-specific strengths and helps mitigate the weaknesses. MPE delivers more than a BPM infrastructure. It helps SMEs to efficiently examine various aspects of BPM and apply the latest developments in their specific environment to achieve high performance. Thus, SMEs clearly need MPE.

The entire MPE approach is relevant for SMEs: based on a process strategy, the design, implementation, execution, and controlling of business processes are required. However, the strategy, especially the business process governance (BPG), can be simplified because of the integration of activities, leading to a "natural" process orientation of SMEs. An identification of processes and their goals in a high-level process model, as well as some basic rules about how to use it in the future is sufficient. However, basic guidelines must be included to define how to use employee integration skills and know-how and efficient decision-making processes to apply BPG principles, as discussed previously. The process controlling can also be achieved more efficiently than in large organizations. This is due to the smaller number of people involved and the lower revenue level, leading to a reduction in the organization's complexity.

The use of reference models plays a key role for small businesses, as we have already seen in the presentation of ARIS SmartPath. However, those models have to include all end-to-end business processes, not just the ERP-based processes or subprocesses. The handling of inter-enterprise processes can be of particular interest in this context. The natural integration and positive attitude of employees makes it relatively easy to adapt SME business processes to best practices documented in reference models. This is supported through the uncomplicated decision-making process. Using reference models significantly increases the efficiency of the process design. This helps to overcome cost and time restrictions in SMEs. It also supports effective training on the job, based on those models, resulting in a solution to the skill and qualification issues.

Change management activities are not as prominent as in large organizations. There are fewer people involved, so information and communication activities are very straightforward, leading to a very resource-efficient approach. The same is generally also true for training, especially if most of it is conducted on the basis of reference models. However, the fact that many people play multiple roles in the training means that efficiency is still crucial. The amount of training per employee may be higher than in large organizations. Some previously discussed, related aspects (e.g., computer-based training) should also be applied in an SME environment.

The SME MPE infrastructure, especially the application IT, can be less sophisticated than in large organizations. The IT support of the process execution is less complex because standardization (e.g., on one ERP system or an SOA architecture with the underlying services) can be achieved more easily owing to size and the decision-making process. In general, there are not hundreds of legacy systems in place that can only be replaced in a long time frame or not at all. In SMEs, the decision to "restart" and simplify IT support can be taken without risking major impacts on the business. Software vendors, such as SAP, Oracle, or Microsoft, offer SME-specific solutions that particularly support the process execution in a small business environment [7–9]. In addition, enhanced solution packages, like the aforementioned ARIS SmartPath (based on standard application software), can be included in the MPE approach. They deliver additional value (e.g., some of the required reference models).

Although applying MPE principles regarding the infrastructure, outsourcing possibilities must be evaluated very carefully. This can extend beyond pure application outsourcing or "software-as-a-service." Processes that handle commodities (e.g., payroll) may be outsourced completely so that limited resources can be focused on the key business processes leading to real competitive advantage. For SMEs, the outsourcing topic can be even more relevant than for large organizations.

The BPM software systems needed to support process governance, and with that, the BPM approach (modeling, monitoring, etc.) are basically the same as those necessary for larger organizations. However, fewer users require considerably less of a software investment. The use of BPM tools, like modeling tools, can also be provided as a service to reduce support issues for SMEs. This must be decided based on the specific situation of an enterprise. However, the outsourcing topic for process design, implementation, and controlling infrastructure is not as significant as in the field of process execution.

MPE, with its approach and philosophy, is an enabler for the success of SMEs and for their attaining high performance. In a small and medium business environment, the approach can be adjusted to the specific characteristics. MPE can become a key enabler for the strengths of SMEs – innovation and agility.

10.4   The Bottom Line

- SMEs are generally defined on the basis of two criteria: revenue and number of employees. One or both criteria must fall under a certain limit (Sect. 10.1).
- SMEs are typically defined in a country-specific manner; for this book, a general definition is applied (Sect. 10.1).
- Although most mid-market organizations have characteristics that challenge the implementation of a BPM approach, they also have attributes that simplify the implementation of such solutions (Sect. 10.1).
- The described characteristics of SMEs have direct impacts on a BPM approach applied in small business (Sect. 10.2).
- BPM solution and software vendors reflect those requirements in holistic solution packages (Sect. 10.2).
- The key deliverables of management of process excellence fit well with the overall characteristics of SMEs (Sect. 10.3).
- Management of process excellence enables the development of SME-specific strengths, helps mitigate the weaknesses, and facilitates the achievement of high performance (Sect. 10.3).
- The use of reference models plays a key role for small businesses (Sect. 10.3).
- Change management activities are not as significant as in large organizations (Sect. 10.3).
- The management of process excellence infrastructure can be less sophisticated than in large organizations; outsourcing can play an important role (Sect. 10.3).

References

1. Wikipedia (ed): Small and Medium Enterprise. In: wikipedia.org (2007)
2. Kirchmer, M: ARIS smartPath – from process design to execution in mid-market organizations. In: Scheer, A-W, Jost, W, Wagner, K (eds.) Von Prozessmodellen zu lauffaehigen Anwendungen – ARIS in der Praxis, pp. 87–98. Springer, Berlin/Heidelberg (2005)
3. Scheer, A-W: ARIS – Business Process Frameworks, 2nd edn. Springer, Berlin/New York/Others (1998)
4. Scheer, A-W: ARIS – Business Process Modeling, 2nd edn. Springer, Berlin/New York/Others (1998)
5. IDS Scheer AG. (ed.): ARIS Platform. Product Brochure. IDS Scheer, Saarbruecken (2007)
6. Kagermann, H, Keller, G: mySAP.com Industry Solutions. SAP Press/Addison-Wesley, London/New York (2000)
7. SAP AG. (ed.): http://www.sap.com/usa/solutions/sme/index.epx (2007)
8. Oracle Inc. (ed.): http://www.oracle.com/applications/jdedwards-enter-prise-one.html (2007)
9. Microsoft Inc. (ed.): http://www.microsoft.com/dynamics/default.mspx (2007)

Chapter 11
What Has Jazz to Do with MPE?

Jazz and MPE have more in common than you may realize. Jazz and its inherent improvisation can be used as a metaphor that helps business process engineers deal with the continuous change and dynamic of today's business environment as they help their organizations pursue high performance. Business process engineers can learn a lot from Jazz musicians.

While working closely with August-Wilhelm Scheer, founder of IDS Scheer, for more than 10 years, I did not just learn a lot about business processes. He also introduced me to the world of Jazz and how it relates to business, which had a major impact on my life. Jazz became my No. 1 hobby. I started learning the piano so that I could understand at least some of the challenges and great skills of many professional musicians. Whenever possible, I listen to live Jazz, at famous clubs like Blue Note, Birdland, Iridium, Smoke or Village Vanguard in New York City, Jazz Showcase in Chicago, the Jazz Bakery in Los Angeles, or Snug Harbor in New Orleans. But I also like to go to smaller, lesser-known Jazz clubs, such as Vincent's in West Chester or Ortlieb's Jazzhaus, and Chris' Jazz Cafe in Philadelphia. I even have part ownership in a jazz club.

The collaboration with Scheer also resulted in a couple of CDs – unfortunately, my musical skills are not sufficient to *play* with the renowned musicians featured on those CDs. However, I acted as the executive producer, organizing the development of all arrangements, bringing the musicians together, booking a recording studio, and seeing the project through to the completion of the engineering work. The CDs are named "Bebop Process Excellence" – Volumes 1 and 2, referring both to "Bebop," an important core Jazz style, and to the notion of Process Excellence.

This title refers to the close relation of Jazz and BPM. A band playing a Jazz tune can be interpreted as a process execution, delivering a result of value for the audience, the customers. They enjoy the tune and pay a cover charge for the music. The sheet music used can be compared to the process models, the "design" of the process of music. The jazz band recording "Bebop Process Excellence – Volume 1" is shown in Fig. 11.1. The band included August-Wilhelm Scheer; Cecil Payne, the famous baritone saxophone player who passed away in December 2007; Mickey Roker, who played in the Dizzy Gillespie Band; and additional recording

Fig. 11.1 Playing a tune is a process; the sheet music is the process model

artists and composers. For the recording of Bebop Volume 2, even Jimmy Cobb, the legendary drummer of the Miles Davis Group that recorded the "Kind of Blue" CD in 1959, joined the performing musicians.

The relation between Jazz and business has numerous facets [1]. An increasing number of professionals use the comparison of Jazz and business for management education in general [2, 3]. This chapter will focus on aspects of Jazz important for MPE. Learning about the principles of Jazz can help one to organize MPE and put the required process governance in place. In working toward particular concepts, such as Enterprise 2.0+, the dynamics and characteristics of a Jazz band and Jazz music become very relevant.

Gold, a musician and educator, distinguishes five key behaviors of jazz musicians that are relevant for business [2]:

- Autonomy: self-governing, independent, and adaptable, but still supporting a larger organization (the band)
- Passion: commitment and energy to pursue excellence
- Risk: ability to take chances and explore new things and to support others in doing so
- Innovation: creating new solutions by finding new ways to recombine existing things
- Listening: ability to really hear and feel the communication of others

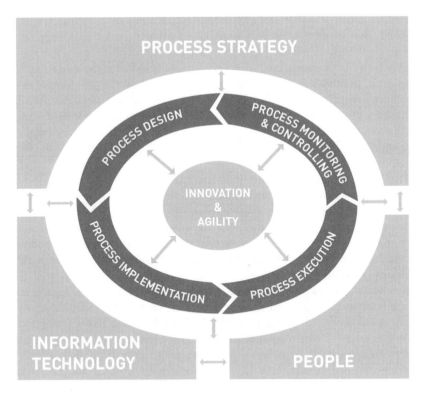

Fig. 11.2 Focus on entire management of process excellence approach

We explore these aspects in the following discussions about Jazz and MPE. This chapter focuses on all aspects of the MPE approach, as shown in Fig. 11.2. It closes the loop from Chap. 1, which introduced the concept of MPE. The principles of Jazz help to set the overall culture for a successful MPE approach. Necessary behaviors and guidelines become clear and can be transferred into the business world. This is relevant for all activities within the MPE approach.

11.1 Teamwork with Continuously Changing Roles

Each musician of a successful and well-performing Jazz band is individually very skilled. This is the basis for the musician's certain level of autonomy. However, to be really successful, the band must work together as a team, toward a joint goal. The melody of a tune is presented by one of the lead instruments and supported by the others. Then, each musician plays a solo, an "improvisation," supported by the rest of the band. After the solo, the musician steps back and supports the next musician in his improvisation. Everyone leads and follows during a Jazz performance.

Naturally, there is a band leader who decides which tunes are played and organizes the band. But during the "process of playing," everyone must lead, support, and follow.

This behavior is coordinated by a very intense informal communication. Brief looks, nods, or other signs enable the band members to exchange information very efficiently and effectively. Musicians listen to one another, so their playing is inspired by the playing of fellow musicians. This results in a very agile team, in which every musician uses their own particular skills to move the entire band – the team – forward to reach its goal of high performance. The band adapts to the overall atmosphere and to the audience.

Traditional companies are still organized like a symphony orchestra. The conductor hands out the sheet music that everyone must play. Then he leads the performance and ensures that everyone follows the plan as defined. All of the other orchestra musicians follow – all the time. They also deliver a result of value, but without the agility of a Jazz band. Top management of a traditional company can be compared with the conductor, and the employees with the musicians of the orchestra.

A modern organization, especially those in industries with a high level of change, such as high tech, must work like a Jazz band to deal with the fast pace of new developments in the business environment. Everyone has to lead efforts in his or her areas of expertise and follow in other initiatives, supporting another leader. This results in high levels of agility and a climate of innovation. The resulting dynamic is especially important for emergent processes, as described previously [1, 4].

Modern organizations are increasingly replacing static organizational structures through the changing roles employees play. MPE provides the framework for the required intense communication and the use of team members' individual skills to achieve overall goals. MPE delivers the basic environment in which the agile business team can truly produce value for clients and enable the organization to become a high-performance business.

Continuous change management is supported by the ongoing intense communication. Every member of a modern company learns from colleagues and provides others with new ideas and know-how, just like musicians in a Jazz band. Change becomes part of the day-to-day routine. This is the business environment required by MPE and ultimately makes BPM a team sport [5].

The changing roles in Jazz bands and enterprises are visualized in Fig. 11.3.

11.2 Find the Right Degree of Freedom

People who are not accustomed to listening to Jazz and its improvisations may think that a musician can just do what he wants during improvisation. But that is not the case. A Jazz tune sets certain parameters, which guide the improvisation. The

Fig. 11.3 Leading and supporting – continuously changing roles

musician must consider the key in which the tune is written, the form, the harmony defined through the chord changes, the rhythm, and the melody.

These parameters define a musician's degree of freedom. If you listen to the classical New Orleans style of Jazz for a few hours, it may become boring. The reason is that the musicians have very little freedom to improvise; the creativity has narrow boundaries. If you listen to Free Jazz for an hour, you may end up with a headache because you do not recognize any structure at all. The musicians have a great degree of freedom – but not much direction. The most interesting and, in my opinion, best-to-listen-to Jazz sets the degree of freedom somewhere in the middle, such as the Bebop style. In this style, musicians have enough freedom to really improvise and be creative while still maintaining harmony, form, and other parameters that makes listening easier and more pleasurable. They have a framework in which they work. They follow a direction that ensures they deliver a result of value to their audience, their customers.

An organization using MPE also must find the right degree of freedom for employees. If every working step is defined in detail through highly refined process models, human creativity is lost and innovation and agility are difficult to achieve. If there are no rules or guidelines, the organization becomes chaos without direction, and is not focused on the company goals. Therefore, companies must set the right degree of freedom when defining business process governance guidelines.

Organizations define the degree of detail to which the business processes should be modeled, and with that, the degree of freedom of the people who must apply and execute them. This can even vary from process to process (e.g., depending on the form of execution – automated or manual). The enterprise architecture defines which aspects of business processes and information systems generally have to be

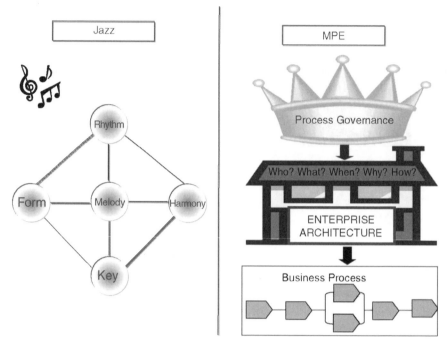

Fig. 11.4 Defining the right degree of freedom

defined and in which format. For example, we discussed the ARIS Architecture [6], requesting the definition of five views on business processes. This sets guidelines for the process implementation and execution with MPE, which in turn ensures the appropriate degree of freedom for the organization's employees. It sets enough direction to reach the defined goals and leaves enough freedom to use all the potential of the involved people. MPE delivers the framework and basic structure for success – while enabling innovation and agility through the right degree of freedom.

The definition of the right degree of freedom in Jazz and business is described in Fig. 11.4.

11.3   Use a Common Language

When a Jazz musician plays a solo, this improvisation is "invented" on the spot. The musician is an "ad hoc composer." However, not everything is invented from scratch. Musicians practice music patterns, or licks, and voicings of chords (e.g., for piano players), which they use during their performances. A lick consists of a certain set of notes that fit well together. Licks are combined to "produce" the improvisation. They can be transferred from one scale to another, from one tune to the next. Every Jazz musician develops a "vocabulary" of music and communicates the tune based on that "language knowledge" during the performance. New musicians start with a limited vocabulary, which they only increase over time. They read the sheet music that visualizes licks and listen to their colleagues to learn the licks.

It is key to use this language of music at the right time during a performance. A Jazz tune has a rhythmical element called "swing" that creates a certain tension. This timing is a main characteristic of Jazz tunes. Every "music communication" must follow that timing. If the tune does not swing during the performance, it is not really Jazz. Jazz musicians communicate and deliver their music under strict time consideration.

Business process engineers also use a specific language. Aforementioned methods (e.g., event-driven process chains) describe processes. Such methods can be used as the basic language of MPE that can be compared to the notes on sheet music for a tune. This language drives the process automation and supports the change management activities – information, communication, and training. Reference models can be compared with the licks Jazz musicians use. They are predefined components that are used to design entire business processes. This supports the agility required by MPE because it ensures an efficient and effective communication based on a common language. New employees can learn from the process documentation and increase their "language knowledge" step by step until they can master the processes in which they are involved.

The timing of process initiatives and related communication is also very important. Enterprises must react quickly, preferably in real time, to changes in the business environment. Information has to be provided in the clearly defined "common language" and in a timely manner. The "real-time enterprise," which is supported through the MPE approach, has to keep the right "swing" using the common "language of BPM," just like a Jazz band. The factor time, combined with effective communication, is just as important for MPE as it is for a Jazz tune.

The use of a common language is visualized in Fig. 11.5.

11.4 Continuous Innovation

During an improvisation, Jazz musicians "invent" new music. As discussed previously, they use existing patterns in the form of licks to put together a new improvisation. This is done in such a way that the audience appreciates the music, and so it is not only something new, but new music that is successfully positioned "on the market." It is a short-term innovation.

In addition, most of the very successful Jazz musicians also contribute to entirely new styles of Jazz. For example, Dizzy Gillespie and Thelonious Monk were at the forefront of Bebop and made this Jazz style a reality [7, 8]. Miles Davis not only heavily influenced Bebop, but was also a driver of Modal Jazz, and later Jazz Rock or Fusion Jazz [9]. Based on their improvisations and strong commitment to

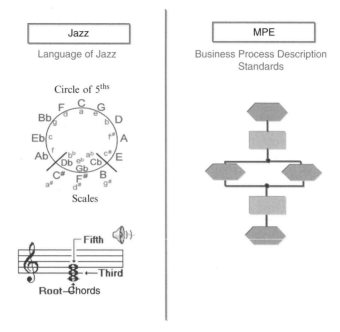

Fig. 11.5 Use of a common language

discovering new musical dimensions, Jazz musicians initiate continuous innovation. In this situation, it is a long-term innovation.

To innovate, Jazz musicians take risks – controlled risks. If someone plays a wrong note, that is generally not a major concern. One can repeat the "mistake" several times and, therefore, make it part of an interesting improvisation, of an innovation, if you will or one can correct the situation quickly by playing a neighboring note that resolves the situation. The high degree of creativity and innovation is possible based on general acceptance of taking the necessary risk and defined approaches to manage risk.

This strong focus on innovation is also a key aspect of MPE. Innovation and agility are the main deliverables. Therefore, MPE requires that people act like Jazz musicians. They must be excited about doing things in a new and better way, about improving processes and inventing new ones. Driving a process from manual execution to semiautomated, then automated, and finally to a flexible, adaptive process can be the key for an organization. Business model innovation based on new processes is very important for many innovation initiatives. MPE needs the Jazz spirit to ensure short-term innovation, as well as long-term innovation effects. That is not something that one can plan and execute in detail. Every employee must practice the appropriate basic behavioral patterns. Everyone must behave and act like a successful Jazz musician, delivering first-class, short-term improvisations and supporting long-term business model changes.

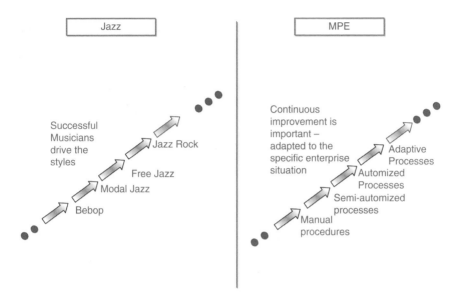

Fig. 11.6 Continuous innovation

An organization must create an environment that encourages taking risks in order to achieve agility and innovation. Innovative companies encourage creativity, even if it increases the risk of mistakes. Tools provided by MPE, such as the approach to managing emergence or the use of simulation and modeling approaches, allow organizations to manage and mitigate this risk.

This also means that the organizational structures in a company must be flexible enough to encourage such innovative behavior. The next-generation enterprise has to be organized like a Jazz band, not like a symphony orchestra. Larger companies may have characteristics of a Jazz Big Band, requiring additional structure, but still offering individuals the freedom to be creative and innovative.

Continuous innovation is illustrated in Fig. 11.6.

11.5   Having Fun Is Important Too

When you listen to live Jazz performances, you can generally feel the excitement and passion of the musicians. You often see that they really have fun doing what they do – improvising, being creative, and taking risks to come up with new, unique ideas. In many cases, this becomes especially obvious in the last set of an evening, when the musicians demonstrate all their talents while feeling good about finalizing a successful performance. "Having fun" is an important basis for delivering good music and for giving the audience the best "result of value." "Having fun" while delivering the "process of music" is a significant aspect of the work of a successful Jazz musician.

Fig. 11.7 Having fun is important, too

That does not mean that playing Jazz music does not require a lot of hard work. Even professional, experienced musicians often practice eight or more hours per day. Having real fun at a performance requires significant effort on the front end. For instance, while learning very basic piano skills, I began to realize how many times I had to practice simple techniques before I could really have fun playing an entire tune.

When I moved from Germany to the United States, an American friend told me that there were two key aspects for being successful in the United States: "funny" and "money." Successful processes should contribute to revenue but it must also be fun to design, implement, execute, and control the processes. Business process engineers and all of the people involved in working on business processes have to like their jobs. They must have a passion for processes and their particularities –and have fun while managing process excellence.

This does not mean that there is no hard work involved. Process engineers have to learn the basic methods and tools to work on processes and be able to apply them successfully in an approach like MPE. Then they can really have fun making things happen and transferring strategic visions into operations.

"Having fun" and "passion" enables creativity and innovation. This leads to the necessary agility of an organization and its members and helps create a culture of innovation. MPE relies on people having fun with their work, resulting in enthusiasm and commitment. That is a precondition for achieving high performance for the business as a whole through a process-centric organization.

This concept is visualized in Fig. 11.7.

11.6   The Bottom Line

- A Jazz band must work together as a team. The members continuously change roles. Everyone leads and follows. This dynamic is also required by Management of Process Excellence, especially for the management of emergent processes (Sect. 11.1).

- Jazz musicians must have enough freedom to really improvise and be creative while still maintaining harmony, form, and other parameters of a tune to make listening easier and more pleasurable. Management of process excellence also has to deliver the right degree of freedom to an organization, especially through the appropriate business process governance (Sect. 11.2).
- Every Jazz musician develops a "vocabulary" of music, a common language. Based on this language, the music must be delivered in the right timing. Management of process excellence uses process models as a language and reference models as the "words" and "sentences." The language of process management must also be used in the appropriate timing (Sect. 11.3).
- Based on their improvisations and the strong commitment to discovering new aspects of their music, Jazz musicians initiate continuous innovation. This is also essential for management of process excellence (Sect. 11.4).
- Having fun and true passion is a significant part of the work of a Jazz musician. It is also essential for management of process excellence. It is important to create a culture of innovation and high performance both in jazz and business (Sect. 11.5).

References

1. Scheer, A W: Epilog: Jazz Improvisation and Management. In: Scheer, A W, Abolhassan, R, Jost, W, Kirchmer, M (eds.) Business Process Change Management – ARIS in Practice, pp. 270–286. Springer, Berlin/New York/Others (2003)
2. Gold, M.: Negotiating Change – Jazz impact – business lecture series. http://www.jazz-impact.com/about.shtml (2007)
3. Wheatland, T.: Jazz in business. http://www.jazzinbusiness.com/engelse%20versie/indexen.htm (2007)
4. Majchrzak, A, Logan, D, McCurdy, R, Kirchmer, M: What business leaders can learn from Jazz musicians about emergent processes. In: Scheer, A W, Kruppke, H, Jost, W, Kindermann, H (eds.) Agility by ARIS Business Process Management. Springer, Berlin/New York/Others (2006)
5. Spanyi, A: Business Process Management Is a Team Sport – Play it to Win! Anclote Press, Tampa (2003)
6. Scheer, A W: ARIS – Business Process Frameworks, 2nd edn. Springer, Berlin/New York/others (1998)
7. Maggin, D: The Life and Times of John Birks Gillespie. HarperEntertainment, New York (2004)
8. De Wilde, L: Monk. Marlowe, New York (1996)
9. Troupe, Q: Miles and Me. University of California Press, Berkeley/Los Angeles (2000)

Epilogue: Process Excellence Is Becoming Popular

The notion of "business process" is no longer just considered an academic topic for experts interested in niche topics. Today, almost every organization, every manager has to deal with business processes, with the management of process excellence (MPE). "Business process" has become part of today's mass culture – at least in the business environment.

Consequently, the concept of "business process" should start getting interesting for artists dealing with topics and images of mass culture. Why should the MPE not become an interesting topic for pop art? We have discussed the relation between jazz and process management, let us finish this book with a brief comment on pop art and process excellence.

Pop art generally involves the use of existing images from mass culture that are already represented in two dimensions, for example, in advertisements, photographs, comic strips, or other mass media sources. Pop art paintings are often emphasizing a flat frontal representation of those popular images and day-to-day life objects. Artists mostly use strong unmixed colors bound by hard edges and suggest a depersonalized approach of mass production. Pop art targets the popular taste sometimes even close to kitsch that was previously considered outside the limits of fine art [1].

You may have heard about well-known pop artists like Andy Warhol, Roy Lichtenstein, Robert Rauschenberg, James Rosenquist, Jasper Johns, Claes Oldenburg, Tom Wesselmann, and Keith Haring [1]. But there are also many more emerging and, in the meantime, more and more accepted artists are dedicated to pop art, such as Romero Britto, James Rizzi, Steve Kaufman, Burton Morris, Peter Mars, and Jeff Schaller [2]. These artists are confronted with a new reality of mass culture.

An important component of the MPE is the transfer of business reality into business process models. These process models and the information technology supporting them during design, implementation, execution, and process controlling have made process management a real mass phenomenon. The depiction of complex business environments in such models also provides a link to pop art by delivering the images that can be picked up by interested artists.

When I discussed this development with Jeff Schaller [3], one of the important emerging pop artists, he got very interested in the topic. The result was the painting

M. Kirchmer, *High Performance Through Process Excellence*,
DOI 10.1007/978-3-642-21165-2, © Springer-Verlag Berlin Heidelberg 2011

Fig. E.1 "Performance Process" by Jeff Schaller

shown on the next page. It is titled *Performance Process* and shows the human element of presses as well as the automation aspects – and in the background the key motivation: to make money. Typical for many pop art pieces is that he even includes a kind of description in the painting. Jeff has really shown that process excellence became popular (Fig. E1).

I hope you enjoy the painting and get interested in getting to know more about process excellence and pop art.

References

1. Livingstone, M.: Pop Art – A Continuous History. Thames and Hudson, London (2000)
2. McKenzie, M.: Images We Love – Popular Art in America. (2003)
3. Schaller, J.: Biography. In: http://www.pinkcowstudio.com/about/bio.html (2008)

Bibliography

American Productivity and Quality Center (APQC): Business process frameworks. On: http://www.apqc.org/process-classification-framework (2011)

Bartlett, C.A., Ghoshal, S.: Managing Across Borders – The Transnational Solution. Harvard Business School Press, Boston (2002)

Becker, J., Schuette, R.: A reference model for retail enterprises. In: Fettke, P., Loos, P. (eds.) Reference Modeling for Business Systems Analysis, pp. 182–205. Hershey, London (2007)

Becker, J., Schuette, R.: Handelsinformationssysteme, 2nd edn. Frankfurt, Redline Wirtschaft (2004)

Becker, J., Knackstedt, R.: Construction and application of for data warehousing. In: Uhr, W., Esswein, W., Schopp, E. (eds.) Wirtschaftsinformatik 2/Band II – Medien – Maerkte – Mobilitaet, Heidelberg (2003)

Blechard, M.: Magic quadrant for business process analysis tools, 2H07-1H08. In: The Gartner Group (ed.) Research Publication G00148777, 6 Aug 2007

Bossidy, L., Charan, R.: Execution: The discipline of getting things done. New York, NY (2002)

Bradly, A., Gootzit, D.: Who's Who in Enterprise 'Mashup' Technologies. In: Gartner Research, ID Number: G00151351, 9 July 2007

Bullinger, H.J., Scheer, A.W.: Service Engineering – Entwicklung und Gestaltung innovativer Dienstleistungen. In: Bullinger, H.-J., Scheer, A..W. (eds.) Service Engineering – Service Engineering – Entwicklung und Gestaltung innovativer Dienstleistungen, Berlin/Heidelberg, e.a. (2003)

Bullinger, H.J., Scheer, A.W. (eds.): Service Engineering – Service Engineering – Entwicklung und Gestaltung innovativer Dienstleistungen, Berlin, (2003)

Carter, S.: The new language of business – SOA & Web 2.0. Upper Saddle River (2007)

Champy, J.: X-Engineering the corporation – Reinventing Your Business in the Digital Age. New York (2002)

Cheese, P., Thomas, R.J., Craig, E.: The Talent Powered Organization – Strategies for Globalization, Talent Management and High Performance. London, (2008)

Christensen, C., Johnson, M.: Business model innovation. Report to the US Council of Innovation. The Conference Board, 01/2007

Christensen, C.M., Raymour, M.: The Innovator's Solution: Using Good Theory to Solve the Dilemmas of Growth. Boston (2003)

Collins, J.: Good to great – Why Some Companies Make the Leap. . .and Others Don't. New York (2001)

Curran, T, Keller, G.: SAP R/3 Business Blueprint: Business Engineering mit den R/3-Referenzprozessen. Bonn (1999)

Davenport, T.: The Coming commoditization of processes. In: Harvard Business Review, June 2005, p. 100–108

M. Kirchmer, *High Performance Through Process Excellence*,
DOI 10.1007/978-3-642-21165-2, © Springer-Verlag Berlin Heidelberg 2011

Davenport, T.: Thinking for a Living – How to Get Better Performance and Results from Knowledge Workers. Harvard Business School Press, Boston (2005)

Davenport, T.: Mission Critical – Realizing the Promise of Enterprise Systems. Harvard Business School Press, Boston (2000)

Davila, T, Epstein, M. J., Shelton, R.: Making Innovation Work. Upper Saddle River (2006)

De Wilde, L.: Monk. New York (1996)

Elzina, D.J., Gulledge, T.R., Lee, C.Y. (ed.): Business Engineering. Norwell (1999)

Exel, S., Wilms, S.: Change management with ARIS. In: Scheer, A.W., Abolhassan, F, Jost, W., Kirchmer, M. (eds.) Business Process Change Management – ARIS in Practice. pp. 23–48. Berlin, New York, and others (2003)

Fettke, P., Loos, P.: Perspectives on reference modeling. In: Fettke, P., Loos, P. (eds.) Reference Modeling for Business Systems Analysis, pp. 1–20. Hershey, London (2007a)

Fettke, P., Loos, P. (eds.): Reference Modeling for Business Systems Analysis. Hershey, London (2007b)

Fettke, P., Loos, P.: Classification of reference models: a methodology and its application. In: Information Systems and E-Business Management, 1(1), pp. 35–53 (2007)

Fettke, P., Loos, P.: Reference models for retail enterprises. In: HMD Praxis der Wirtschaftsinformatik, pp 15–25. 235, (2004)

Fingar, P.: Extreme Competition – Innovation and the Great 21st Century Business Reformation. Tampa (2006)

Fleisch, E., Christ, O., Dierkes, M.: Die betriebswirtschaftliche Vision des Internets der Dinge. In: Fleisch, E., Mattern, F. (eds.) Das Internet der Dinge – Ubiquitous Computing und RFID in der Praxis, pp. 3–37. Heidelberg, Berlin (2005)

Fleisch, E., Mattern, F. (eds.): Das Internet der Dinge – Ubiquitous Computing und RFID in der Praxis. Springer, Heidelberg/Berlin (2005)

Fleischmann, A.: Subject-oriented Business Process Management. White Paper, Muenchen (2007)

Franz, P.: Prioritizing Process Improvements to maximize Business Agility. Accenutre Point of View document, London (2011)

Franz, P., Kirchmer, M., Rosemann, M.: Value driven Business Process Management – Which values matter for BPM. Accenture, Queensland University of Technology (QUT) White Paper, London, Philadelphia, Brisbane (2011)

Friedman, T.L.: The World Is Flat – A Brief History of the Twenty-First Century. New York (2005)

George, M. L.: Lean Six Sigma for Service – Conquer Complexity and Achieve Major Cost Reductions in Less than a Year. New York (2003)

George, M., Works, J., Watson-Hemphill, K.: Fast Innovation – Achieving Superior Differentiation, Speed to Market, and Increased Profitability. McGraw-Hill, New York (2005)

George, M.L., Wilson, S.A.: Conquering Complexity in Your Business – How Wal-Mart, Toyota and Other Top Companies Are Breaking Through the Ceiling on Profits and Growth. New York (2004)

Global360 (ed): www.global360.com (2007)

Gold, M.: Negotiating Change – Jazz Impact – Business Lecture Series. In: http://www.jazz-impact.com/about.shtml (2007)

Greenbaum, J.: SimEnterprise: The video gamer's guide to SAP's business-process revolution. In SAP Netweaver Magazine, vol. 2, (2006)

Hammer, M.: Six steps to operational innovation. In: Harvard Business School Working Knowledge for Business, hbswk.hbs.edu (2005), 30 Aug 2005

Hammer, M.: The Internet and the Real Economy. Documentation of Sapphire 99. Philadelphia (1999)

Hammer, M., Stanton, S.: The Reengineering Revolution. Harper Collins, Glasgow (1995)

Hammer, M., Champy, J.: Reengineering the Corporation. HarperBusiness, New York (1993)

Harmon, P.: A new type of activity. In: Business Process Trends (ed.) Newsletter, vol. 5, Number 19, 11/2007

Harmon, P.: Business Process Change Management – A Manager's Guide to Improving, Redesigning, and Automating Processes. Morgan Kaufmann, San Francisco (2003)

Hess, H., Blickle, T: From Process Efficiency to Organizational Performance. ARIS Platform Expert Paper. Saarbruecken 3/07

Heuser, L., Alsdorf, C, Woods, D.: International Research Forum 2006 – Web 2.0 – IT Security – Real World Awareness – IT as a Tool for Growth and Development. New York (2006)

Heuser, L., Alsdorf, C, Woods, D.: Enterprise 2.0, The Service Grid, User-Driven Innovation, Business Model Transformation – International Research Forum 2007. New York (2008)

IDS Scheer AG (ed.): ARIS Platform. Product Brochure. Saarbruecken (2007)

IDS Scheer AG (ed.): ARIS Design Platform – ARIS Enterprise Architecture Solution. White Paper. Saarbruecken 3/2006

Imai, M.: Kaizen – Der Schluessel zum Erfolg der Japaner im Wettbewerb. 8. Auflage, Muenchen (1993)

IQPC (ed.): Proceedings of the Business Process Management Summit, Las Vegas 10/2007

Johnson, M., Suskewicz, J.: Accelerating Innovation. In: Pantaleo, D., Pal, N.: From Strategy to Execution – Turning Accelerated Global Change into Opportunity. Berlin e.a. 2008, pp. 49–64

Jost, W.: Vom CIO zum CPO. In: Harvard Business Manager, 9/2004

Jost, W.: EDV-gestuetzte CIM Rahmenplanung. Wiesbaden (1993)

Jost, W, Scheer, A.W.: Business process management: a core task for any company organization. In: Scheer, A.W., Abolhassan, F., Jost, W., Kirchmer, M.: Business Process Excellence – ARIS in Practice. Berlin, New York, and others, pp. 33–43. (2002)

Kagermann, H., Keller, G.: mySAP.com Industry solutions. London/New York (2000)

Kalakota, R., Robinson, M.: Service Blueprint: A Roadmap for Execution. Addison-Wesley, Boston (2003)

Kalakota, R., Robinson, M.: M-Business – The Race to Mobility. McGraw-Hill, New York (2002)

Kalakota, R., Robinson, M.: E-Business – Roadmap for Success. Peachpit Press, Berkeley and others (1999)

Kaplan, R., Norton, D.: The Balanced Scorecard – Translating Strategy into Action. Harvard Business School Press, Boston (1996)

Kirchmer, M.: The Process of Process Management: Delivering the value of Business Process Management. Accenture Point of View Document, Philadelphia (2011)

Kirchmer, M.: Competitive Advantage is an end of Change: 11 Typical situations where Business Process Management delivers Value. Accenture Point of View Document. Philadelphia (2011)

Kirchmer, M: Process innovation through open BPM. In: Pantaleo, D., Pal, N. (eds.) From Strategy to Execution – Turning Accelerated Global Change into Opportunity. Berlin pp. 87–105. (2008)

Kirchmer, M.: Knowledge communication empowers SOA for business agility. In: The 11th World Multi-Conference on Systemics, Cybernetics and Informatics, July 8–11, 2007, Orlando, Proceedings, vol. III, pp. 301–307. (2007)

Kirchmer, M.: Business Process Governance: Orchestrating the Management of BPM. Whitepaper, Berwyn, PA (2005)

Kirchmer, M.: ARIS SmartPath – From process design to execution in mid-market organizations. In: Scheer, A.W., Jost, W., Wagner, K. (eds.) Von Prozessmodellen zu lauffaehigen Anwendungen – ARIS in der Praxis. Berlin, p. 87–98. (2005)

Kirchmer, M.: E-business process networks – successful value chains through standards. In: Journal of Enterprise Management, vol. 17 No. 1, (2004)

Kirchmer, M.: e-Business process improvement (eBPI): Building and managing collaborative e-Business scenarios. In: Callaos, N., Loutfi, M., Justan, M. (eds.) Proceedings of the 6th World Multiconference on Systemics, Cybernetics and Informatics. Orlando, vol. VIII, pp. 387–396. (2002)

Kirchmer, M.: Market- and product-oriented definition of business processes. In: Elzina, D.J., Gulledge, T.R., Lee, C.-Y. (eds.) Business Engineering. Norwell, pp. 131–144. (1999)

Kirchmer, M.: Business Process Oriented Implementation of Standard Software – How to Achieve Competitive Advantage Efficiently and Effectively. 2nd edn. Berlin, New York and others (1999)

Kirchmer, M., Gutierrez, F., Laengle, S.: Process Mining for Organizational Agility. Industrial Management January/February 2010

Kirchmer, M., Spanyi, A.: Business Process Governance. Whitepaper, 2nd revised edn. Berwyn (2007)

Kirchmer, M., Scheer, A.W.: Business process automation – combining best and next practices. In: Scheer, A.W., Abolhassan, F., Jost, W., Kirchmer, M. (eds.) Business Process Automation – ARIS in Practice. Berlin, New York, and others, pp. 1–15. (2004)

Kirchmer, M., Scheer, A.W: Change management – key for business process excellence. In: Scheer, A.W., Abolhassan, F., Jost, W., Kirchmer, M. (eds.): Business Process Change Management – ARIS in Practice. Berlin, New York, and others, pp. 1–14. (2003)

Kirchmer, M., Brown, G., Heinzel, H.: Using SCOR and other reference models for e-business process networks. In: Scheer, A.W., Abolhassan, F., Jost, W., Kirchmer, M. (eds.) Business Process Excellence – ARIS in Practice. Berlin, New York, and others, p. 45–64. (2002)

Kirchmer, M., Enginalev, A.: Internationales informationsmanagement – aufbau von informationssystemen im internationalen verbund. In: Zentes, J., Swoboda, B.: Fallstudien zum Internationalen Management. Wiesbaden, pp. 717–729. (2000)

Kraemer, W, Gallenstein, C, Sprendger, P.: Learning management fuer fuehrungskraefte. In: Industrie Management – Zeitschrift fuer industrielle Geschaeftsprozesse, pp. 55–59. (2001)

Kraemer, W, Mueller, M.: Virtuelle corporate university – executive education architecture and knowledge management. In: Scheer, A.-W (ed.) Electronic Business und Knowledge Management – Neue Dimensionen fuer den Unternehmenserfolg. Heidelberg, pp. 491–525. (1999)

Lapkin, A.: The seven fatal mistakes of enterprise architecture. In: Gartner Research publication, ID-Number: G00126144, 2/22/2005

Livingstone, M.: Pop Art – A Continuous History. Thames and Hudson, London (2000)

Lochmaier, L.: Management 2.0 und der intelligente Schwarm. In: manager-magazin.de (2007)

Maggin, D.: The Life and Times of John Birks Gillespie. Harper, New York (2004)

Majchrzak, A., Logan, D., McCurdy, R., Kirchmer, M.: Four keys to managing emergence. In: MIT Sloan Management Review, Winter, vol 47, no. 2. (2006)

Majchrzak, A., Logan, D., McCurdy, R., Kirchmer, M.: What business leaders can learn from jazz musicians about emergent processes. In: Scheer, A.W., Kruppke, H., Jost, W., Kindermann, H. (eds.) Agility by ARIS Business Process Management. Berlin, New York, and others (2006)

Matter, E.: Die technische Basis fuer das Internet der Dinge. In: Fleisch, E., Mattern, F. (eds.) Das Internet der Dinge – Ubiquitous Computing und RFID in der Praxis, pp. 39–66. Springer, Heidelberg/Berlin (2005)

McAffee, A.: Enterprise 2.0: The dawn of emergent collaboration. In: MIT Sloan Management Review, vol. 43 no. 3, Spring (2006)

McGovern, J., Ambler, S.W., Stevens, M.E., Linn, J., Sharan, V., Jo, E.K.: A Practical Guide to Enterprise Architecture. Prentice Hall, Upper Saddle River (2004)

McHugh, P., Merli, G., Wheeler, W.: Beyond Business Process Reengineering – Towards the Holistic Enterprise. Chichester, New York (1995)

McKenzie, M.: Images We Love – Popular Art in America. (2003)

Melenowsky, M. J.: Business Process Management as a Discipline. Gartner Research, 08/2006

Microsoft, Inc. (ed.): http://www.microsoft.com/dynamics/default.mspx, (2007)

Microsoft, Inc. (ed.): Your Business – Connected. BizTalk. In: Microsoft.com (2007)

Newman, D.: BPM & SOA: Real world stories of business success. In: IQPC (ed.) Proceedings of the Business Process Management Summit, Las Vegas, October 2007

Nolan, T., Goodstein, L., Pfeiffer, J.W.: Plan or die! 10 Keys to Organizational Success. Pfeiffer, San Diego (1993)

Oleson, J.: Pathways to Agility – Mass Customization in Action. Wiley, New York/Chichester (1998)

Oracle, Inc. (ed.): http://www.oracle.com/applications/e-business-suite.html (2007)

Oracle, Inc. (ed.): http://www.oracle.com/applications/jdedwards-enterprise-one.html (2007)

Oracle, Inc. (ed.): Oracle Fusion – Next Generation Applications. oracle.com (2007)

O'Reilly, T: What is Web 2.0 – Design Patterns and Business Models for the Next Generation of Software. www.oreilly.com (2005)

O'Rourke, C., Fishman, N., Selkow, W.: Enterprise Architecture using the Zachman Framework. Thomson Course Technology, Boston (2003)

Pantaleo, D., Pal, N.: From Strategy to Execution – Turning Accelerated Global Change into Opportunity. Springer, Berlin (2008)

Pegasystems (ed.): www.pega.com (2007)

PMOLink (ed.): Project Management Processes – Based on the PMBOK Guide. New Orleans (2004)

Porter, M.: What is strategy? Harvard Bus. Rev. (1996)

Porter, M.: Competitive Strategies: Techniques for Analyzing Industries and Competitors. Free Press, New York (1998). originally published in 1980

Recker, J., Rosemann, M., van der Aalst, W., Jansen-Vullers, M., Drelling, A.: Configurable reference modeling languages. In: Fettke, P., Loos, P. (eds.) Reference Modeling for Business Systems Analysis, pp. 22–46. Hershey, London (2007)

Reilly, B., Hope-Ross, D., Knight, L.: Marketplaces and process mediation – the missing link. In: Gartner Group (Ed.): Research Note 19 September 2000. Rummler, G.; Brache, AL: Improving Performance: Managing the White Space on the Organization Chart. Jossey-Bass (1990)

Robinson, M., Kalakota, R.: Offshore Outsourcing – Business Models, ROI and Best Practices. Mivar Press, Alpharetta (2004)

Runyan, G.: Logistics marketplaces: Shaping the evolution of BtoB commerce. In: The Yankee Group (Ed.) BtoB Commerce & Applications Report. vol.5, no. 13, (2000)

SAP AG (ed.): http://wwwll.sap.com/usa/solutions/business-suite/erp/index.epx (2007)

SAP AG (ed.): http://www.sap.com/usa/solutions/sme/index.epx (2007)

SAP AG (ed.): SAP NetWeaver Helps Put You Ahead of the Curve. In: sap.com (2007)

SAP AG (ed.): SAP Info – Quick Guide: SAP NetWeaver – The Power of Lower TCO, p. 40. (2003)

Schaller, J.: Biography. In: http://www.pinkcowstudio.com/about/bio.html (2008)

Scheer, A.W.: Epilog: Jazz improvisation and management. In: Scheer, A.W., Abolhassan, R., Jost, W., Kirchmer, M. (eds.) Business Process Change Management – ARIS in Practice. Berlin, New York, and others, pp. 270–286. (2003)

Scheer, A.W.: Start-Ups Are Easy, But... Berlin, New York (2001)

Scheer, A.W. (ed.): Electronic Business und Knowledge Management – Neue Dimensionen fuer den Unternehmenserfolg. Heidelberg (1999)

Scheer, A.W.: ARIS – Business Process Frameworks, 2nd edn. Springer, Berlin, New York, and others (1998)

Scheer, A.W.: Business Process Engineering – Reference Models of Industrial Enterprises, 2nd edn. Springer, Berlin (1994)

Scheer, A.W., Jost, W., Guengoez, O.: A reference model for industrial enterprises. In: Fettke, P., Loos, P. (eds.) Reference Modeling for Business Systems Analysis, pp. 167–181. Hershey, London (2007)

Scheer, A.W., Kruppke, H., Jost, W., Kindermann, H.: Agility by ARIS Business Process Management. Springer, Berlin, New York, and others (2006)

Scheer, A.W., Jost, W., Wagner, K.: Von Prozessmodellen zu lauffaehigen Anwendungen – ARIS in der Praxis. Springer, Berlin, Heidelberg (2005)

Scheer, A.W., Abolhassan, R., Jost, W., Kirchmer, M. (eds.): Business Process Automation – ARIS in Practice. Springer, Berlin, New York, and others (2004)

Scheer, A.-W, Abolhassan, R, Jost, W, Kirchmer, M. (ed.): Business Process Change Management – ARIS in Practice. Berlin, New York, and others 2003, p. 1–14

Scheer, A.W., Abolhassan, R, Jost, W, Kirchmer, M. (ed.): Business Process Excellence – ARIS in Practice. Berlin, New York, and others 2002

Scheer, A.W, Habermann, R, Koeppen, A.: Electronic business und knowledge management –
     Neue Dimensionen fuer den Unternehmenserfolg. In: Scheer, A.-W. (ed.) Electronic Business
     und Knowledge Management – Neue Dimensionen fuer den Unternehmenserfolg. Heidelberg
     1999, pp. 3–36
Snee, R., Hoerl, R.: Leading Six Sigma – A Step-by-Step Guide Based on Experience with GE and
     Other Six Sigma Companies. Upper Saddle River, New York, e.a. (2003)
Spanyi, A.: More for Less – The Power of Process Management. Meghan-Kiffer, Tampa (2006)
Spanyi, A.: Business Process Management is a Team Sport – Play it to Win! Meghan-Kiffer,
     Tampa (2003)
Spath, D., Baumeister, M., Barrho, T., Dill, C.: Change management im Wandel. In: Industrie
     Management – Zeitschrift fuer industrielle Geschaeftsprozesse, 4/2001, pp. 9–13
Stolz, H.: Composite Applications Framework – Designing Cross Solutions. In: SAP AG (ed.):
     SAP Info – Quick Guide: SAP NetWeaver – The Power of Lower TCO, 4/2003, p. 40
Supply Chain Council (ed): Supply Chain Operations Reference Model – Plan, Source, Make,
     Deliver, Return. Version 8.0, 2007
Troupe, Q.: Miles and Me. Berkley, 2000
Value Chain Group (ed.): Business Process Transformation Framework. In: www.value-chain.org
     2007
Van Belle, J.: Evaluation of selected enterprise reference models. In: Fettke, P., Loos, P. (eds.)
     Reference Modeling for Business Systems Analysis. Hershey, 1997, p. 266–286
Wahlster, W, Dengel, A.: Web 3.0:Convergence of Web 2.0 and the Semantic Web. In: Techno-
     logy Radar Feature Paper, Edition 11/2006, Germany June 2006
Wheatland, T: Jazz in Business. In: http://www.jazzinbusiness.com/engelse%20versie/indexen.
     htm 2007
Widener University, School for Business Administration: Business Process Innovation. At: www.
     widener.edu 5/2007
Wikipedia(ed.): Blog. In: www.wikipedia.org 12/2007
Wikipedia (ed.).: Small and Medium Enterprise. In: wikipedia.org 12/2007
Wikipedia.(ed.): Web 2.0. In: www.wikipedia.org 12/2007
Wikipedia (ed.): Business Process Execution Language. In: wikipedia.org 12/2007
Wikipedia (ed.): Web 2.0. In: wikipedia.org, 12/2007
Williams, L.: E-Markets: How BtoB marketplaces are creating a commerce operating system.
     In: The Yankee Group (ed.) BtoB Commerce & Applications Report. vol.5, no. 11 (2000)
Williams, L.: Corporate-sponsored vs. independent BtoB exchanges: who will win? In: The
     Yankee Group (Ed.) BtoB Commerce & Applications Report. vol.5, no. 12 (2000)
Woods, Dan: Enterprise Service Architectures. Beijing/Cambridge/Koeln, and others 2003
Woods, D.: Packaged Composite Applications. O'Reilly, Beijing/Cambridge/Koeln (2003). and
     others
Woods, D., Mattern, T.: Enterprise SOA – Designing IT for Business Innovation. O'Reilly,
     Beijing/Cambridge (2006)
Zentes, J., Swoboda, B.: Fallstudien zum Internationalen Management. Gabler, Wiesbaden (2000)